IMPROVING CHILDREN'S LEARNING

Every teacher will be interested in performing to the best of his or her abilities in today's climate of targets and tables. Much research over recent years has focused on the role of the teacher and how effective classroom practice is achieved.

The book discusses many areas of topical importance including teaching methods; motivating learners and matching work to children; how best to structure children's learning; classroom control and organisation; teaching literacy; teaching children with special educational needs and working with parents.

It also looks at the increasing role of the teacher as researcher and how collaborative working practices are providing a way for teachers to appraise the progress both of themselves and of their colleagues. This book should be of particular interest to the classroom teacher who is looking for ways to develop his or her teaching and has limited time to explore the research. It sets out to translate the findings of research into practical terms which teachers can easily use.

Joan Dean has been a head teacher, senior primary adviser and chief inspector during her years in education. She has published widely in the field and is the author of four other titles for Routledge. In 1980 she was awarded the OBE for services to education.

EDUCATIONAL MANAGEMENT SERIES
Series editor: Cyril Poster

Recent titles in this series include:

MANAGING DISCIPLINE IN SCHOOLS
Sonia Blandford

THE PRIMARY SCHOOL IN CHANGING TIMES:
THE AUSTRALIAN EXPERIENCE
Edited by Tony Townsend

SCHOOL CHOICE AND COMPETITION:
MARKETS IN THE PUBLIC INTEREST?
Philip Woods, Carl Bagley and Ron Glatter

CHOICE AND DIVERSITY IN SCHOOLING:
PERSPECTIVES AND PROSPECTS
Edited by Ron Glatter, Philip Woods and Carl Bagley

MANAGING INFORMATION TECHNOLOGY IN SCHOOLS
Roger Crawford

CONTINUING PROFESSIONAL DEVELOPMENT
Anna Craft

SUCCESS AGAINST THE ODDS
The National Commission on Education

MANAGING SPECIAL NEEDS IN THE PRIMARY SCHOOL
Joan Dean

MANAGING THE PRIMARY SCHOOL (2ND EDN)
Joan Dean

THE SKILLS OF PRIMARY SCHOOL MANAGEMENT
Les Bell and Chris Rhodes

EDUCATION FOR THE TWENTY-FIRST CENTURY
Hedley Beare and Richard Slaughter

MAKING GOOD SCHOOLS: LINKING SCHOOL EFFECTIVENESS
AND SCHOOL IMPROVEMENT
Edited by Robert Bollen, Bert Creemers, David Hopkins, Louise Stoll and Nijs Lagerweij

INNOVATIVE SCHOOL PRINCIPLES AND RESTRUCTURING
Clive Dimmock and Tom O'Donoghue

THE SELF MONITORING PRIMARY SCHOOL
Edited by Pearl White and Cyril Poster

MANAGING RESOURCES FOR SCHOOL IMPROVEMENT:
CREATING A COST EFFECTIVE SCHOOL
Hywel Thomas and Jane Martin

SCHOOLS AT THE CENTRE: A STUDY OF DECENTRALISATION
Alison Bullock and Hywel Thomas

DEVELOPING EFFECTIVE SCHOOL MANAGEMENT
Jack Dunham

MEETING THE CHALLENGES OF PRIMARY SCHOOLING
Edited by Lloyd Logan and Judyth Sachs

RESTRUCTURING AND QUALITY IN TOMORROW'S SCHOOLS
Edited by Tony Townsend

THE ETHICAL SCHOOL
Felicity Haynes

IMPROVING CHILDREN'S LEARNING

Effective teaching in the primary school

Joan Dean

London and New York

First published 2000
by Routledge
11 New Fetter Lane, London EC4P 4EE

Simultaneously published in the USA and Canada
by Routledge
29 West 35th Street, New York, NY 10001

Routledge is an imprint of the Taylor & Francis Group

© 2000 Joan Dean

Typeset in Garamond by
Florence Group Ltd, Stoodleigh, Devon
Printed and bound in Great Britain by
MPG Books Ltd, Bodmin

British Library Cataloguing in Publication Data
A catalogue record for this book is available
from the British Library

Library of Congress Cataloging in Publication Data
Dean, Joan.
Improving children's learning : effective teaching in
the primary school / Joan Dean.
p. cm. — (Educational management series)
Includes bibliographical references and index.
(pbk. : alk. paper)
1. Elementary school teaching—Great Britain. 2. Elementary
school teachers—Training of—Great Britain. 3. Effective
teaching—Great Britain. I. Title. II. Series.
LB1725.G6D43 2000
372.1102—dc21 99–31129
CIP

ISBN 0–415–16896–1

CONTENTS

1 Introduction   1

2 Assessing research   6

3 The children   9

4 The teacher   24

5 The classroom climate   38

6 Effective teaching and learning   51

7 Classroom management   75

8 Working in groups   92

9 The teaching of literacy   101

10 The teaching of mathematics   120

11 Exceptional children   129

12 Working with parents   139

13 Evaluation and record keeping   152

14 The teacher as researcher   166

15 Conclusions   171

Bibliography   175
Index   185

1

INTRODUCTION

Debbie Johnson taught at Merefield primary school, a one form entry school where she had a class of thirty-three Year 3 children. She was in her fourth year of teaching and thoroughly enjoyed her work. She provided a great deal of first-hand experience for her children. They made many visits and she often brought things into the classroom to show them. Learning was usually an active process but carefully structured so that children were able to work independently and find things out for themselves without going down too many wrong turnings. Project work was an important part of the programme. Sometimes projects were subject specific which gave an opportunity to explore in depth and sometimes they were cross-curricular which helped children to see links between subject areas and practise the skills they were learning in one subject in others. Projects were planned over the year so that there was a balance in the kinds of studies which were undertaken. The school also gave a good deal of thought to the continuity from year to year and all the teachers knew the subjects of the projects being undertaken in each year group.

A lot of the work in Debbie's class was individual. In mathematics, for example, children worked through a carefully planned programme at their own pace for part of the time but this was carefully balanced with some whole-class and small group work. Debbie made a lot of use of children's own ideas, particularly for writing, and work often stemmed from something a child had brought into school, when she might encourage the child to investigate further. There was a good deal of creative work of all kinds. Children drew and painted and made three-dimensional models to a high standard. Debbie kept good records of individual work and it was the practice in the school for teachers to write a review of any topic work they had undertaken and to discuss this with the headteacher.

Debbie's work might be described as following the pattern suggested by the Plowden Report (Central Advisory Council for Education 1967). As such it was successful in many ways. Delamont (1987) describes the Plowden view as follows:

It celebrates self-expression, individual discovery, first-hand experience, discovery learning and personal growth . . . it emphasises the process of learning rather than its products; and it offers a relatively high degree of choice (though still somewhat circumscribed) in the type, content and duration of activities.

(Delamont 1987: 186)

It has been fashionable in recent years to decry the philosophy of the Plowden Report. We seem to have forgotten that before the Plowden Report thoughtful teachers adopted the kinds of practice which came to be advocated in Plowden because they were dissatisfied with what we now think of as traditional practice. They saw in this approach a way of working which enabled them to cater more effectively for children's different abilities and needs. It also has to be remembered that much of what Plowden advocated is still important today. For example, the following paragraph is highly relevant to present day society:

For such a society, children, and the adults they will become, will need above all, to be adaptable and capable of adjusting to their changing environment. They will need as always to be able to live with their fellows, appreciating and respecting their differences, understanding and sympathising with their feelings. They will need the power of discrimination and, when necessary, to be able to withstand mass pressures. They will need to be well-balanced, with neither emotions nor intellect giving ground to each other. They will need throughout their adult life to be capable of being taught, and of learning, the new skills called for by the changing economic scene. They will need to understand that in a democratic society each individual has obligations to the community, as well as rights within it.

(Central Advisory Council for Education 1967: 185, para. 496)

It has also been shown in many studies that while teachers in primary schools were much influenced by the Plowden Report, many did not adopt in full the practice it advocated, preferring to adopt certain aspects while retaining what they saw as being good in traditional practice. What has happened, however, is that many teachers attempted the impossible in trying to teach children as individuals in classes which were too large to allow this. This meant that the attention they could give to any child was limited and that work which might more effectively have been done on a class basis was attempted with individuals. Current thinking suggests that the balance of whole-class and individual work needs to be adjusted. Ofsted (1996: 30) suggests that 'Too often teachers do not vary their methods sufficiently . . . The majority of good lessons consist of a blend of direct teaching to the whole class, to groups and individuals so that teaching closely matches their existing attainment and builds on it.'

It has also been the case that children in primary schools, though normally seated in groups, do little work on cooperative group basis, though many teachers use ability groups as a way of dealing with the spread of ability within their classes, especially in schools too small to have a class for each age group.

The National Curriculum has also made for considerable changes in the way teachers work. The curriculum has become much broader and it is to be hoped that the recent emphasis on literacy and numeracy will not make teachers revert to a narrower curriculum. At the same time the National Curriculum and the programme of testing at the end of Key Stages have put pressure on teachers and there is less time to pursue interests which arise. Woods (1995) found that, while the teachers in his study welcomed the broadening that the National Curriculum brought, they regretted the fact that it left them less time to respond to children's initiatives. The most confident teachers felt less constrained by the National Curriculum than their colleagues.

Raven et al. (1985), in describing work which crosses subject boundaries, make the point that there are many skills and qualities which are important parts of the educational process which are fostered by the kind of broad project work which the best of primary schools have practised in the past. Their book starts with a description of the headmistress of a small primary school, who is the teacher of a mixed age class, describing the important human qualities she thinks education should be concerned with in addition to academic learning:

> These other qualities included leadership, the ability to work with others, creativity, the ability to communicate, and the ability to muster an argument. They also included the ability to pursue an interest single-mindedly, the ability to follow effectively, and the ability to contribute to group processes. They included self-reliance and confidence in dealing with others. They included self-discipline and willingness to contribute to activities in which the well-being of others was dependent on what one did. They included willingness to take responsibility for doing what was necessary to ensure the well-being of the community. They included artistic and aesthetic skills and sensitivities, and sensitivity to the overall effects of materials intended to communicate effectively.
>
> (Raven et al. 1985: 1)

Many writers give lists of the characteristics of effective schools and teachers, for example Beare et al. (1989), Edmonds (1979), Purkey and Smith (1985), Scheerens (1992), Sammons et al. (1995). Stoll and Fink (1996: 28) choose to define a school as effective if it:

- promotes progress for *all* of its pupils beyond what would be expected given consideration of initial attainment and background factors;
- ensures that each pupil achieves the highest standards possible;
- enhances all aspects of pupil achievement and development;
- continues to improve year to year.

Stoll and Fink state that 'School effectiveness research also suggests that classroom actions account for more of the variation in schools' effects on pupil outcomes than does school level activity' (p. 48).

The following are findings made by various researchers about effective teachers:

- Effective teachers prepare well and have clear goals for their teaching.
- They aim to make as much teaching contact with all their children as possible.
- They aim to see that children spend as much time profitably on task as possible.
- They have high expectations for all children.
- They make clear presentations which match the level of the children.
- They structure work well and tell children the purpose of the work they are doing and the targets they hope the children will achieve.
- They are flexible in varying teaching behaviour and activities.
- They use many higher order questions which demand thinking on the part of the children.
- They give frequent feedback to children about how they are doing.
- They make appropriate use of praise for both achievement and behaviour.
- They keep good records of the attainment and progress of individual children and these are shared and used. Progress in learning is constantly assessed.
- Their classrooms are well-organised, ordered and attractive.
- They reflect on the work they and the children have done and evaluate progress towards goals.

Galton (1995: 106) suggests that 'expert' teachers 'tend, more than their colleagues, to view classroom events from the pupils' perspective as well as their own'. Woods (1995: 2) writes of creative teachers and how they overcome constraints:

> They are inevitably constrained by systems and structures externally determined, but creative teachers can, to some extent, affect the situations in which they work, applying their talents to changing or modifying the circumstances and increasing the range of opportunities. They cannot do this without a large measure of

commitment to the values they espouse, and strong motivation, and indeed, inspiration, in seeing them implemented.

This book sets out to look at what research has found to be effective for children's learning at the primary stage. These findings provide useful guidelines for teachers reflecting on their work in the classrooms.

2

ASSESSING RESEARCH

There is now a substantial body of research about school effectiveness and school improvement and in reading this you need to read critically, being aware of ways in which to judge the relevance of the research to your own situation. Anyone reading this research needs to ask questions about the text:

1   *What is the sample of schools/teachers chosen? Does it include different types of schools? What age groups does it deal with? What generalisations can be made from it?*

Many studies have been made in areas which are socially disadvantaged because these schools give more cause for concern. This needs to be remembered in generalising from the results. A large number of studies have been made in other countries and while we can learn from them differences in the culture need to be taken into account.

2   *What criteria of effectiveness have been chosen?*

A number of studies have simply used tests in the basic skills and these may be lower order skills rather than skills requiring creativity and higher level of thinking. The more useful studies have also been concerned with affective and social development and matters such as children's self-esteem and self-confidence.

Romberg and Carpenter (1986: 862) make the following comment about the use of standardised tests in research about teacher effectiveness: 'As long as teachers choose the contents they emphasise in their classroom, such tests can never be used as fair measures of teacher effectiveness because they evaluate students in areas that the teacher did not cover or emphasise.'

It is also important that a range of criteria are used. For example, Rutter *et al.* (1979) used examination results, attendance, behaviour and delinquency in their study of secondary schools. Mortimore *et al.* (1988) used reading, mathematics (written), mathematics (practical), writing, speaking, attendance, behaviour and a range of attitudes in their study of primary schools. They also used measures of the socio-economic status of the parents.

3 *What measures of the children's background have been used?*

Many of the studies of school effectiveness have arisen from concern that schools do not start equal because children come from different backgrounds, some of which are more supportive of school work than others. Reynolds and Reid (1985: 195) sum this up as follows: 'Outcomes cannot merely be seen as being produced by effective or ineffective schools without an assessment of which pupils, from which families and for which communities they are held to be effective or ineffective.'

4 *What is the time element in the study?*

Some studies are simply measures at one point in time. Others look at progress over a period. Effective schools need to be effective over time. A school may obtain good results one year but poor results the next. Year groups vary and it is the ability to obtain good results over time that is important.

Some researches are concerned with progress as well as achievement, for example Mortimore *et al.* (1988). This gives a different point of view and is a better measure of a school's work than achievement alone.

5 *What research techniques have been employed?*

There will be some statistical information obtainable from the school, for example, attendance figures, Standard Attainment Tasks (SATs) results and teacher assessment. Studies may also include observation of classroom and management practice, examination of children's work, testing of various kinds, questionnaires to children, teachers and parents, interviews with teachers, children and parents, action research with and by teachers, case studies and any other ideas the researchers may have. It is important that more than one method is used so that information from one source of information reinforces another. For example, studies relying on questionnaires may fail to ask questions which turn out to be important and those responding may fail to give information which might be important. Questionnaires need to be backed up with other information.

It is also important that studies are valid and reliable. Validity is the extent to which a test or observation measures what it is intended to measure. Reliability is the extent to which the same results will be obtained if the measure is repeated.

6 *What methods of analysis have been used?*

The methods of analysis should make it possible to provide information about the ways that measures are related. However, it is important not to assume that when two measures are highly correlated that one is the cause of the other. For example, there is usually a correlation between the number of free school meals in a school and children's achievement, but it would be ridiculous to claim that reducing the number of free school meals would improve performance.

Most modern research uses highly sophisticated statistical techniques which allow different factors to be isolated.

7

7   *Do several studies draw similar conclusions?*
    Evidence is more convincing if it is confirmed by more than one researcher.
8   *Is there any contrary evidence?*
    Different researches will come up with slightly different conclusions and
it is useful to ask whether several studies come to similar conclusions. It
is also worth considering whether the findings accord with your experience
and that of other teachers.

Some researches have found that schools have different effects on different
pupils. Nuttall *et al.* (1989), for example, found differences with respect to
gender and ethnic background. They also found that some schools narrowed
the gap between the most and least able, and others widened it. Schools
are not uniformly effective over all areas of curriculum since these reflect
differences in teaching ability. Some primary schools will be more effective
with some age groups than with others and this too will be a reflection on
teachers.
    Ouston and Maughan (1985: 33) note the importance of the hidden
curriculum, 'the assumptions, values, attitudes and behaviour of pupils and
teachers are not in evidence in the formal curriculum. These are, almost by
definition, difficult to measure, yet they seem likely to play a major part
in explaining why some schools are more successful than others.'
    Education, like other aspects of our world, does not stand still. The possi-
bilities of new technology may make tomorrow's schools almost unrecog-
nisable and they may need different qualities from those which research is
showing to be effective at present.

3

THE CHILDREN

Children have a culture of their own which is different from that of the school and the culture of the classroom you are developing as the teacher. It is also a part of the classroom climate. It is concerned with how to live with one's peers, how to react to them, how to manage the fact that there is a continuous evaluation of children going on both by the teacher and by other children. There will also be cultures within groups of children within the class.

Pollard (1985: 47) suggests that:

> A number of social skills are involved [in being competent within the children's culture], including how to gain entry to group activities, how to express oneself and act when with one's peers and how to manage conflicts successfully – in short, how to be a 'member' of a group of friends, who can maintain and act on the shared meanings and understandings that have been constructed.

Some children will find difficulty in acquiring these skills and may need your help in relating to peers. The children's culture provides norms and constraints for children which they have to learn to manage.

Becoming a person

Children are in the process of becoming persons. Pring (1988: 44) suggests that:

> What is distinctive about personhood is the consciousness not only of others but of oneself – a sense of one's own unity as a person, one's own value and dignity, one's own capacity to think through a problem, to persevere when things get tough, to exercise a platform of values and beliefs, whereby one can exercise some control over one's destiny.

He also writes of 'the capacity to think, to reflect, to make sense of one's experience, to engage critically with the received values, beliefs and assumptions that one is confronted with' (p. 43) as being part of personhood. You need to consider how these capacities are developed in children and to look for opportunities to help children to reflect on experience.

Children need a measure of security if they are to develop. Within the classroom they need to know:

- what the teacher expects of them;
- how to get the teacher's approval;
- what they may and may not do;
- where they may or may not go;
- what they may or may not use;
- when they may or may not do certain things.

A person in an insecure situation works to achieve security. The right amount of insecurity provides motivation for learning but too much may prevent a child from taking risks for fear of incurring your displeasure. Children are especially likely to feel insecure when they come into a new situation whether this is a new school or simply a new class. Until they find out what is expected of them they are likely to be anxious and it is important that you work to make them more secure as quickly as possible.

Feeling secure is closely related to self-esteem. A person feels insecure when his or her self-esteem is put at risk. Low self-esteem may motivate if children feel that they can change the situation so that they can succeed. However, a threat to self-esteem may make children feel helpless, simply blaming others for their failure so that their self-esteem is protected.

Children gradually come to experience the effect of competition even if you work hard to avoid the disadvantages of a competitive atmosphere in the classroom. Fontana (1988: 88) describes how children become aware of their own performance relative to that of other children. 'In the infant school, the child becomes very conscious that certain levels of performance are expected of him by his teachers, and he begins to compare his own efforts at achieving these levels with the kind of success met by other children.'

He goes on to say that if he is unsuccessful he may 'either show a passive acceptance of it and a disinclination to try new things in the future, or he may rebel against it and show a rejection of all the school activities that remind him of it' (p. 88).

This all points to the importance of matching work to children and to trying to see that all children experience a measure of success.

Moral development

During their primary years children are beginning to develop a moral sense. Young children take on and internalise the precepts of their parents and teachers as being the rules for doing right or wrong and are rewarded with affection and approval when they conform to these and with disapproval when they do not. These precepts become part of the child's developing conscience. Gradually children begin to develop a personal moral sense arising from their interaction with others and the extent to which they are able to reflect on experience.

You can influence the extent to which children make such reflection by the way in which you deal with incidents which occur in the classroom and playground from day to day. For example, the way you deal with mis-behaviour and aggression may help children to learn how to manage situations that arise more thoughtfully and with greater skill. Children need to be helped to think through what has happened and to envisage a better way of acting particularly where this concerns relationships with others.

Braddy (1988: 161) lists the following aims for moral education with young children:

- to provide opportunities for children to make choices in everyday situations;
- to develop strategies with children for problem solving;
- to develop techniques with children for resolving conflict situations;
- to encourage the children to be aware of their own intentions and the intentions of others;
- to provide opportunities for children to exercise responsibility and trust.

You will also want to include helping children to recognise and accept and follow the moral precepts which our society believes to be important. Much of this learning will take place in the course of day-to-day living in the classroom and you need to use opportunities as they arise for discussion about moral ways of behaving.

The Berkshire County Council document on personal and social educa-tion *Pathways to Life* (1997: 9) lists a number of core values which schools should be concerned to promote. They are 'tolerance, respect, personal responsibility, development of self-worth and self-esteem, recognition of others' contributions and worth, fairness and justice, willingness to acknow-ledge others' points of view, empathy, co-operation, consideration for other people and for the environment'.

Some schools and classes use what is known as 'circle time' to discuss problems which children are encountering in their day-to-day experience and to think together about ways of solving such problems. Many of the problems will be to do with relationships and the discussion will be concerned with alternative ways of acting. Wooster (1988: 206) suggests that this activity might start with individual children responding briefly to such topics as 'A time I felt really happy', 'A time I felt really angry' 'A time when I felt really scared'. He suggests that the group might brain-storm ideas about anger, for example, looking for ways of dealing with feeling angry. Discussion might then turn to planning and goal setting.

Wright (1985: 139) suggests that 'morality is between persons in the sense that it represents the ideal way in which relationships between persons should be regulated'. He also suggests that 'the irreducible heart of morality is to be found in a limited number of core ideas, not in a set of rules of behaviour' (p. 139). These core moral ideas he lists as follows: 'respect for persons, fairness and justice; truthfulness; and that of keeping promises and contracts which is essential to all community life and cooperative activity' (p. 140).

The self-concept

Part of becoming a person is the development of the self-concept. Children gradually acquire a view of themselves from interaction with others, both adults and other children. The self-concept is thus something which is learned from other people's reactions. Your contribution as teacher is thus particularly important in the formation of the self-concept in that your views carry author-ity. You therefore need to be very conscious that quite minor comments on your part can have a considerable effect on a child's self-concept and self-esteem. It is also important that you ensure that every child, as far as possible, achieves success. This means taking care that work is well matched to individuals. Gurney (1990: 8, 9) goes on to say that 'a pupil who develops low self-esteem will lose confidence and take the blame for failure (even though it may not be his fault)' and 'the basic view that the child has of himself . . . will be resistant to change once it is established'.

Schunk (1990) writes of the way that children attribute success or failure to different causes such as ability, effort, task difficulty or luck and the effect this attribution has on the effectiveness with which the child operates and thus on the self-concept. Young children tend to attribute success to effort and as they grow older they attribute it more to ability. This influences their expectation of success and the role of effort declines in importance. Schunk makes the point that 'Pupils frequently compare their performance with those of their peers, and feel more (less) efficacious when they believe they are accomplishing more (less) work. Peers are important models and observing models is a form of social comparison' (p. 78).

Schunk also notes that 'Persuader credibility is important because pupils may experience higher efficacy when told they are capable of learning by a trustworthy source (for example, the teacher) whereas they may discount the advice of less credible sources' (p. 78).

He also reports research which showed that children who received feedback on ability with teachers commenting that a child was good at something did better than children who received feedback on effort such as a comment that a child had been working hard.

Gurney (1990: 16) suggests that extra-curricular activities may offer a very useful contribution to children's self-esteem. 'The pupil is a volunteer and therefore wants to learn, the atmosphere is more relaxed, group size is usually smaller and teachers may be keener.' He also suggests that teachers should praise children for making positive statements about themselves.

Docking (1992: 79) notes that

'Self-esteem is clearly affected by many factors, but the following appear to be particularly important:

● having the opportunity to succeed;
● appreciating your own success;
● believing that others value you; and
● having a strong sense of identity.

As a teacher you are in a very powerful position in relation to these points. Docking also suggests that 'What is needed is a challenge which is beyond the pupil's current levels of achievement but also within their grasp' (p. 79). He suggests that children can be encouraged to make a list of things they are good at, including out-of-school activities, and revise it from time to time.

Cooper and McIntyre (1996: 22) suggest that:

The extent to which pupils see the outcomes of their classroom activities and of their schooling generally, as depending on their abilities, on their own efforts, on their choice of strategies, on the actions and judgements of their teachers or on other factors such as 'luck' is probably a very important influence on their learning.

Age differences

Mortimore et al. (1988: 123) found that teachers tended to ignore differences in the age of children. Teachers tended to think that children were less able when in fact they were simply younger. 'Summer-born children were consistently more likely to be judged as below average ability than were their autumn term counterparts.' They found that the month of birth was significantly related to writing performance. 'Variations in the length (in words) of children's writing were also related to age. This difference, when account was taken of other factors, remained highly significant in all years' (p. 122). The gap in attainment remained highly significant and did not increase or decrease with age. Children's performance in number work was also affected by age.

They also found that 'Teachers also listened to autumn-born children read more frequently than they listened to their younger peers, even though the older children scored more highly in the reading assessment and were rated as being of higher ability' (p. 164). Less than a third of the teachers reported that they gave younger and older pupils different work in language and mathematics.

The effect of all this was that the younger children had less favourable views of school. 'Thirty-one per cent of the youngest (summer-born) group had an unfavourable view of mathematics compared to only 19 per cent of the oldest (autumn-born). Thirty-seven per cent of summer-born, compared with only 28 per cent of autumn-born pupils had a negative view of school' (p. 127).

This problem is particularly evident in small schools where a class may contain children of different year groups.

The effect of social background

Mortimore *et al.* (1988: 132) also found that there was a strong relationship between social class and achievement. 'A gap of nearly ten months in reading age was found between children with fathers in professional or intermediate non-manual work and those with fathers in unskilled manual work.' This relationship between social class and achievement remained throughout the time the children spent in the junior school and increased as the children grew older. In reading there was also a correlation with progress as well as achievement. In mathematics there were social class differences at entry to junior school, but these did not increase with time and were not related to progress.

Tough (1973) is reported by Tizard (1975: 5, 6) as finding that:

> In professional families, the mother encourages the child to make comparisons, to recall the past and to anticipate the future, to offer explanations, and look for differences; she reads him stories, encourages creative indoor activities and imaginative play. Because the working-class child has had less of these kinds of experience he enters school with a different set of meanings and does not respond in the way which the teacher hopes to the tasks she sets him. Her response is usually to decide that 'his language is poor' and to try to extend his vocabulary and syntax. What he needs, however, is help in the development of verbal thinking skills.

14

The teachers are to be encouraged not simply to listen to the child with interest or to 'chat' with him, but to help the child to ask questions, solve problems, explore the meaning of particular situations, and in general to use language as a means of learning.

Tizard and Hughes (1984), on the other hand, studied thirty pre-school girls with their mothers at home, half of whom were from middle-class and half from working-class families. They found that all the mothers spent time talking to their children and both middle-class and working-class mothers asked and answered questions with their children. They talked about the past and future and discussed people and things which were not present. Children were frequently given information about colour, size and number and also information which might be classified as general knowledge. They found 'no significant social class difference in the number of conversations, the length of conversations, or the number of word in either mothers' or daughters' "turns" of talk' (p. 139). 'All the mothers made comparisons, offered explanations, used "if . . . then" constructions, and linked events in time, and all but one used language for recall and to discuss the future' (p. 141).

The differences they found were as follows (p. 148):

> The middle-class mothers discussed a larger range of topics with their children than the working-class mothers. A significantly larger proportion of their conversations were concerned with topics that went beyond the 'here and now'. That is, they more often talked to their children about people who were not present, and about past and future events. Further, a larger proportion of their talk was concerned with conveying information to the children and they gave their children more of the kind of information we classified as 'general knowledge' (science, history, geography).

They went on to study the same children in nursery school where they found that the levels of conversation were much more limited than the children were experiencing at home. Teachers there also tended to underestimate the working-class children who asked fewer questions than the middle-class children, talked less to teachers and tended to ask for help in dealing with other children more frequently than the middle-class children. 'The effect of these characteristics was to make the working-class girls appear particularly unassertive, subdued and immature at school. The middle-class girls, whose behaviour was much less affected, thus appeared noticeably more assertive, at ease and confident' (p. 219).

Mortimore *et al*. (1988: 138) also found that social class had an effect on the way teachers assessed their children, which persisted even when the actual results indicated that the differences were less than the teachers assumed.

There were very marked differences, according to father's social class, in the percentage of pupils rated by their class teachers as above or below average. In the autumn of the second year [Year 4] 48 per cent of the non-manual, compared with only 25 per cent of the semi- and unskilled manual group were rated as of above average ability. Only 16 per cent of the non-manual but 32 per cent of the semi- and unskilled manual group were rated as below average ability. By the third year [Year 5] the differences were even greater.

Teachers tended to have a slightly more favourable view of those from non-manual backgrounds. Thus higher teacher expectation may be a factor which contributes to the greater progress in reading and writing made by the non-manual group in comparison with other groups during the junior years.

This evidence all suggests that teachers need to question themselves a good deal about their assumptions about working-class children.

Gender differences

There are behavioural differences between girls and boys from a very early stage. Whyte (1988: 153) makes the following observation:

> In both sexes, the tendency to conform to conventional sex-role behaviour is exaggerated when others are present. In a study set in a playroom, it was found that children who had played with cross-sex toys (boys with dishes and dolls, girls with trucks and aeroplanes) abandoned them in favour of a sex-appropriate toy when another child entered their play space.

He also found that play becomes more sex-stereotyped as children grow older. Boys use more constructional play and play with bricks, cars and trains and girls use the wendy house/home corner and dolls' house more (p. 154).

Girls and boys develop at different rates and boys at the primary school stage tend to develop more slowly than girls. Sammons and Mortimore (1990: 139) found the following differences in reading ability in their study of London junior schools:

> Only 17 per cent of girls, compared with 33 per cent of boys, obtained scores in the bottom quartile of the distribution at entry to junior school. In contrast, 31 per cent of girls, compared with 19 per cent of boys obtained scores in the top quarter of the distribution. At the end of the third year [Year 5], 19 per cent of girls

obtained scores in the bottom quarter. Moreover, 31 per cent of girls and only 21 per cent of boys obtained scores in the top quarter of the distribution.

They found that 'girls did not make greater or less progress in reading over the junior years than boys' (p. 149).

The situation was similar where writing was concerned. Girls outstripped boys to a significant degree in the length of their writing and in its quality and ideas. The situation was somewhat different in mathematics where there was no significant difference although there was a slight but not significant difference in favour of the girls at the end of Year 5. Girls made slightly more progress than boys during the junior school years. There was no evidence that girls had a less positive view of mathematics than boys.

Tizard *et al.* (1988) found that teachers tended to assess girls' abilities as being lower than boys'. They noted that from the age of about 4 girls show greater anxiety about failure than boys and are more sensitive to negative information. Sammons and Mortimore also found that in spite of the fact that girls outperformed boys to a considerable extent, teachers' assessments of their children tended to favour the boys although the difference was not significant.

They found that girls also had more positive self-concepts in relation to school than boys in all years but 'sex differences in attitude to curriculum were weak or non-existent' (p. 144). Boys were less likely than girls to rate themselves highly for anxiety. Mortimore *et al.* found that boys were also consistently assessed as having more behaviour difficulties. They also found that teachers 'communicated more on an individual level with boys than with girls' (p. 167). They also heard them read more often.

A number of studies show differences in the way teachers treat boys and girls. Kelly (1988) reviewed research, mainly American, into gender differences in teacher/pupil interaction. She concluded that, on average, the studies found that girls receive 44 per cent of all classroom interactions and boys receive 56 per cent. Girls received only 35 per cent of criticisms, of which only 32 per cent were concerned with behaviour. They received 44 per cent of questions, 44 per cent of response opportunities and 48 per cent of praise. Girls were more likely to volunteer answers than boys.

Croll (1986) also found that boys received more attention than girls but concluded that to some extent this was explained by the fact that more boys than girls have special educational needs. Girls with special needs also received greater attention but there were also boys who did not have special needs who received more attention than girls. Croll reports that no studies found that girls received more attention than boys.

Galton and Simon (1980) found that girls tended to have more anxiety than boys but they were more contented with school and 'more strongly motivated to do their best and please the teachers' (p. 159).

These findings all suggest that you need to be very sensitive to the way you treat boys and girls. The fact that teachers apparently make fewer critical comments to girls suggests that there is a sensitivity to girls' reactions to negative comments. It may be salutary to note the way opportunities to respond are distributed during a discussion session. Just being conscious of the possibility that boys receive more than their fair share of your attention may help to right the balance. There may also be good reasons for an imbalance which teachers feel subconsciously and react to.

Ethnic differences

Teachers in many schools have children from a variety of cultural backgrounds in their classes. Houlton (1988: 23) suggests that teachers need:

> A grasp of the key features of the cultural systems of the main ethnic groups living in Britain. At a minimum level these include awareness of languages spoken, religious beliefs, names and naming systems, dress styles and dietary habits. For teachers in close contact with ethnic minority groups a much larger data base may be needed.

He goes on to suggest that this might include rules of etiquette, value systems, customs and traditions, child-rearing practices and family structures. He also makes the point that teachers need to be aware of their own attitudes towards ethnic minorities.

Mortimore *et al.* (1988) report that children of Caribbean and Asian backgrounds made significantly poorer progress in reading than other groups but there was no evidence of ethnic effects on progress in mathematics. There were differences in reading ability which were linked to the children's home language. Gujerati speakers were better readers than Punjabi speakers.

There was a tendency for Asian, Caribbean and Turkish children to produce shorter pieces of writing by the third year (Year 5) but if writing was assessed in terms of its quality rather than its length, children from ethnic backgrounds did as well as other groups.

Sammons and Mortimore (1990: 149) note that 'there was a higher incidence of behaviour difficulties in school (according to class teachers' assessment) amongst the Caribbean children than amongst other groups'. These were mainly related to learning difficulties. 'In each year, children of Caribbean background were present for a higher percentage of the time than the English group, whilst children of Asian backgrounds were, on average, absent for a higher percentage of time' (p. 150).

Social relationships

Children starting school, whether from home or pre-school provision, have a great deal to cope with in social terms. Cleave (1988: 49, 50) notes that the child has to adapt to the following:

- being in a crowd, particularly in the playground;
- the presence of fewer adults or unfamiliar adults at playtime and dinner time;
- organisational processes such as lining up, queuing or waiting;
- competition for adult attention. This involves waiting and fewer opportunities for one-to-one conversation than has been possible at home or in a pre-school group;
- being addressed as one of a group or class;
- restrictions on movement and noise;
- organisational constraints on time with the possibility of being last or left behind.

As a teacher you will be concerned with the way in which children relate to each other. An important part of learning in school is how to get on with other people and the way you organise work in the classroom may or may not contribute to developing this skill. Children learn social skills through their friendships and you can help children who find difficulty in making friends by talking to them about the skills of getting on with other people. Maxwell (1990: 184) makes the following points about this:

> If one of the main aims of school is to encourage the development of pupils into well-adjusted, socially competent adults, then the social life of the classroom has to be given consideration by teachers. It should include fostering appropriate relationships in the group and facilitating constructive group activity between friends, and the rooting of educational experiences designed to promote social and moral development in the context of children's day-to-day social experience with their own friends.

The Elton Report on discipline in schools (DES 1989a: 241) found that 'In the course of their duties around the school, the vast majority of primary teachers reported pupils showing a lack of concern for others.' Docking (1992: 91) suggests that 'Children can gradually learn to become less aggressive towards each other if they are encouraged to reflect upon their emotions and reactions to situations in which they would ordinarily hit out physically or verbally.'

Needham (1994: 162) describes a class where the children looked at role-playing playground situations like 'how to join in a game; how to refuse entry to a game without causing upset; how to resolve playground conflicts without asking the teacher on duty to intervene.'

Maxwell notes that there appears to be a relationship between having a close friend and social sensitivity to the feelings of other people. He also suggests that teachers should use friendship groupings when possible. On the other hand, studies of group work (e.g. Bennett and Dunne 1992, Wheldall and Glynn 1989) tend to find that children work more effectively in groups of mixed gender while friendship groups tend to be children of the same sex. Group work is one of the ways in which children can learn social skills and the evidence is that while most primary classes seat children in groups, the amount of actual group working together that goes on is limited. Group work will be looked at in greater detail in Chapter 8.

Brier (1988: 126) writes of the need for children to develop 'the ability to be sensitive to one's own and to others' feelings' and suggests that the teacher's aim should be 'to help children to learn that different people feel differently, feelings change and it is possible to identify this through listening, looking and talking'. She also suggests that 'extending children's thinking and thereby their "behaviour vocabulary" offers them a wider range of behaviours from which to choose their action; they are thus helped to become effective in coping with the interpersonal relationships and events which they encounter daily' (p. 124).

Gurney (1990: 19) notes that 'Pupils often feel frightened or guilty of their strong negative feelings towards, say, a parent or a sibling. These can be progressively aired over a period of time, initially on a generalised basis.' Story writing can offer a good opportunity for children to write of their feelings through a description of how a fictional character felt.

Views of the curriculum

The PACE project (Primary Assessment, Curriculum and Experience) (Broadfoot and Pollard 1996) interviewed fifty-four children asking for their views of the subjects they liked and disliked. Physical education came top of the list in Years 1 and 2 and mathematics in Year 2 and technology in Years 3 and 4. The project is still working through the primary school and work with years 5 and 6 will be reported later.

Children generally liked tasks at which they were successful and which they found easy. This was more true in Years 3 and 4 than in Years 1 and 2. Interest came next and then fun. Very few gave educational reasons for liking work.

Years 3 and 4 saw teachers as choosing what they did virtually all the time whereas the younger children saw themselves choosing more or sharing choice with the teacher. Children generally felt they got on well with their teacher and there were very few negative replies to this question. Girls tended to be more positive than boys. They tended to grow more negative about teacher evaluation as the years went on.

Pollard (1996c: 128) reports 'Whilst there is considerable awareness of the importance of the appearance of the work and of the need to be correct, there is little sense that the pupils were alert to more educational criteria which their teacher might use.'

Goal setting

There is much to be said for setting goals for children or helping them to set goals for themselves. This helps them to see their own progress as they achieve each goal. There are advantages in children working in pairs to set goals which they can monitor for each other. Goals need to be specific where possible, so that it is easy to see when they have been achieved. Schunk (1990) describes a study in which half the children in a class were given goals for each session of an instructional programme designed to teach division. Children in the other half of the class were just advised to work productively. The class was also divided in half again and half were given information about the number of problems that other similar children had completed and the other half were given no such information. The children who received both goals and comparative information did better than the other children.

Schunk also suggests that 'goals that incorporate specific performance standards are more likely to raise learning efficacy because progress towards an explicit goal is easier to gauge' (p. 81). He also notes that goals which are close at hand result in greater motivation than more distant ones.

The national project in numeracy requires teachers to give each child an individual conference of about ten minutes each term at which progress is discussed and up to three targets set to be achieved by the next conference. The targets should be recorded and copied to parents so that their support is gained.

Racism

Gaine (1987) found that teachers in primary schools where there were few children from ethnic minorities tended to doubt that racist attitudes existed in young children. He suggests that this is partly because they have not 'examined their own assumptions about race, immigration, and prejudice, so that the things pupils say may simply not grate on their ears the way they would on others' (p. 10). In a later book (1995: 72) he suggests that when teachers explore their children's thinking they tend to see things differently. He suggests that the aim should be 'for people not to be categorised by something like skin colour but to receive equal treatment as individuals'.

The Swann Report (DES 1985c: 236) makes the following comment about attitudes in schools:

A major conclusion which we feel must regrettably be drawn from the findings of this project, is in relation to the widespread existence

21

of racism, whether unintentional and 'latent' or overt and aggressive in the schools visited. The project revealed widespread evidence of racism in all the areas covered, ranging from unintentional racism and patronising and stereotyped ideas about ethnic minority groups combined with an appalling ignorance of their cultural backgrounds and of the facts of race and immigration, to extremes of overt hatred and 'National Front' style attitudes.

Teachers, especially those in 'white' areas need to discuss together the way they should achieve the aim given above with all their children. The process of discussing this and the production of a school policy does much to clarify issues and helps people to think out what their own views may be.

Gurnah (1987: 15) found that black parents 'believe that a lot of teachers hold stereotypes of their children which not only divide them from white children but also from children from other black communities'. He also notes that 'Black parents have not found schools sufficiently friendly to wish to get involved with them as parents or governors.'

All schools need a policy for multicultural education which deals with racism. Teachers need to look at their curriculum from a multicultural point of view. They also need to investigate the views that children hold. Gaine suggests that it can be salutary to give children a sheet of paper and tell them that they are sitting at home watching television when there is a knock at the door. When they go to answer it there is a black man or a Pakistani or a Chinese girl. The children then write about what happens then. His finding in undertaking this study is that 'Typically between fifty and sixty per cent of the class will write something signifying a sense of threat, hostility or perceived strangeness' (p. 6).

The Select Committee on Race Relations and Immigration (1980–81) stressed the need for all schools to prepare children for life in an ethnically diverse society, whether or not they had ethnic minority pupils on roll. They suggest that through ethos and curriculum schools should promote understanding and respect among all pupils for the different ethnic groups who now contribute to our national life.

Developing pupil autonomy

Schools should be aiming to help children to become autonomous learners. All children should leave school able to learn without a teacher and the primary school should do much to place children on the road to this goal. Holt (1994: 8) notes that 'One of the most important things teachers can do for any learner is to make the learner independent of them.' Kutnick (1990: 119) suggests that this should be carefully planned and not left to chance. He points out that 'knowledge is constructed through joint activity

and discourse. Adults and peers each have unique and overlapping contributions to make to this development.'

Webb and Vulliamy (1996: 46) suggest that helping children to become
independent learners 'involved sharing the purpose behind tasks with
children and helping them to understand and contribute to the criteria by
which their work would be judged'. They suggest asking questions about
finished work such as 'What do you think of it?' 'What do you like about
it?' 'How could you make it better?' Evaluation sheets asking what went
well and what did not were another suggestion.

As a teacher you need to work to make children independent learners.
They should be encouraged to ask questions and to seek out answers rather
than being dependent all the time on knowledge coming from you. This
means seeing that children have many first-hand experiences, learn to
observe, ask questions of people who might know the answers, learn to
hypothesise, sort out information and learn from each other through
discussing what they have discovered. They also need to learn to use the
Internet to find things out. Your use of questions may also have an influence.
Teachers who ask questions which make children think – possibly questions to which they do not have a straightforward answer – help children
to become more independent thinkers. Studies of the questions teachers ask
suggest that they ask far more questions which are simply a matter of recall
than questions which demand independent thought.

4

THE TEACHER

To be a teacher is like living a life dedicated to a mission impossible. To begin to satisfy the complex demands loaded onto teachers by government, parents, employer, children and society at large is unthinkable. Even if the demands were compatible and flexible it would take several lifetimes of schooling to achieve them and social change would make some aspects of the tasks obsolete even before they were attempted. Yet despite this, the satisfaction of teaching can be immense. No other profession can experience the immediate joy of children's new learning, understanding and fulfilment or see the long-term results of the commitment, enthusiasm and careers that are found in school.

(Eggleston 1992: 1)

He goes on to list key teacher skills:

- Trying to ensure that one discovers the capabilities of all children.
- Taking care that one's judgements are not influenced by negative expectations about social class, gender or race.
- Building upon what capabilities the children already have, never suggesting that what they bring (especially in the way of language) is valueless.
- Remembering that differences established or reinforced in school may determine almost all aspects of a child's future and, collectively, play a large part in determining future social structure.

(Eggleston 1992: 6)

Cullingford (1995: 19) notes that:

A survey of children asking them to identify the skills they most admired in a teacher found that the greatest virtue was the ability to explain, to clarify issues, and demonstrate how to understand them. This explaining included factors such as patience and not humiliating the children.

Nias (1989: 180) surveyed the views of a large number of primary teachers about the work they did. She found that the large majority were committed to their work and found considerable personal satisfaction in it. She notes that 'When teaching is conceptualised as a relationship between two or more people, rather than as an instrumental activity, it becomes possible for teachers to find personal and emotional satisfaction in their working lives rather than outside them.'

Teaching style

Every teacher has a personal style. You start to develop your style as soon as you start teaching and to begin with you tend to reflect the styles of teachers you have observed, both as a pupil and as a student teacher. It is important that newly qualified teachers have good opportunities for observing other teachers so that they can use them as models, selecting aspects of style which they feel fit the way they would like to teach.

Your style results partly from your personality, partly from your experience, partly from your philosophy and values and partly from the context within which you are working. As you grow in experience, you become more confident and your style becomes more pronounced. You learn the things which work for you and the things which create problems. Most teachers have quite strong views about the work they are doing and the way in which primary education should be carried out and these affect the style they adopt. You will also be constrained to some extent by the school in which you are working. If your colleagues all work in very formal ways you will find it difficult to work informally, especially if the head obviously approves of formal teaching. The children will take a long time to adapt to informal working and you are likely to adapt your approach to take all this into account. The converse would also be true.

Your style is evident in the way you present material to children, the way you use time, the degree of flexibility you allow yourself and the children, the way you organise work, your relationship with the children, your communication, the degree of freedom you allow the children and many other things. These are all areas which you need to reflect upon.

There have been a number of studies of teaching style. An early study by Neville Bennett (1976) compared teachers who use formal teaching methods with others who used informal methods. His formal teachers tended to teach separate subjects whereas the informal teachers integrated the curriculum. The formal teachers used external rewards and placed emphasis on memory, practice and rote learning with regular testing. The informal teachers taught mainly by discovery with an emphasis on cooperative group work and creative work. A number of teachers used mixed methods with some elements of both formal and informal approaches.

He compared the results using tests of basic skills and two essays, one on 'What I did at school yesterday' and 'Invisible for the day'. On the test of basic skills the teachers who used formal or mixed methods came out better than those who used informal methods. In the essay writing both formal and informal groups did equally well and the mixed methods groups slightly less well. There was no evidence that the informal classes were worse at spelling and grammar.

However, low-achieving boys did better in informal classes and the most successful class was taught by informal methods but the work was highly structured. He found that 'Pupils in formal classrooms engage in more work-related activity, irrespective of the level of initial achievement, the discrepancy being particularly large at low and high achievement levels' (p. 108).

This study has been criticised on the grounds that the sample was comparatively small (37 classes) and the formal teachers were more experienced. The tests used also tended to favour formal teaching methods.

The Oracle study (Galton and Simon 1980 and Galton *et al*. 1980) defined teaching styles and children's learning styles and related them. They defined teaching styles as follows:

- *Individual monitors* Teachers who tended to work mainly with individual children. Interactions tended to be brief and the teachers were under pressure. These teachers represented 22.4 per cent of the sample.
- *Class inquirers* These teachers used a good deal of questioning and made more statements of ideas and problems than others. They were 15.5 per cent of the sample.
- *Group instructors* These teachers spent more time than others on working with groups and less time on individual work. This allowed them to spend more time on questioning and making statements. They represented 12.1 per cent of the sample.
- *Style changers* These teachers represented 50 per cent of the sample and showed a mixture of the other three styles. 'They ask the highest number of questions related to task supervision, make more statements of critical control and spend more time hearing children read than do teachers using the other styles' (p. 124). They divided into three sub-groups – infrequent changers who changed styles during the course of the year; rotating changers who rotated pupils from one group to another; and habitual changers who made regular changes between class and group instruction.

Learning and teaching styles

Pollard and Tann (1987: 154) state that 'a "learning style" can be described as the way an individual typically approaches a learning situation and it derives from a mix between an individual's cognitive processes and their personality'. They quote Beech (1985) who suggests that there is some evidence that at least 40 per cent of primary children tend to be visualisers rather than verbalisers and can translate what they read or hear into their mind's eye. As a teacher you need to study individual learning styles and the way children work and consider their implications for the way in which you deal with individual children. It helps to discuss with individuals how they set about their work. You can also encourage children to visualise as a way of helping them to remember.

The Oracle study also identified pupils' learning styles and related them to teaching styles. There were four learning styles which were as follows:

- *Attention seekers* They 'either cooperate on task or routine work for 66.6 per cent of the time. They either seek or are the focus of most of the teacher's contact with individuals' (p. 143). They frequently leave their places to make contact with the teacher. They represent 19.5 per cent of the sample.
- *Intermittent workers* 'They have the lowest levels of interaction of all four clusters. They have, however, the highest levels of contacts with other pupils . . . Although these pupils are working for 64.4 per cent of the time, they are also involved in some form of distraction during one fifth of the observation periods' (p. 145). They represent 35.7 per cent of the sample.
- *Solitary workers* These pupils receive very little attention from the teacher and show reluctance to interact with other pupils. They tend to be passive during class discussion but spend a higher proportion of time on their set tasks than any other group (77.1 per cent). They tend to remain fairly static. They represent 32.5 per cent of the sample.
- *Quiet collaborators* These pupils interact with the teacher as part of a group or class audience. They have the second highest level of work interaction and engage in relatively little interaction amongst themselves. They represent 12.3 per cent of the sample.

'Nearly 50 per cent of the pupils taught by *individual monitors* . . . were in the group that worked intermittently, while at the other extreme the *class inquirers* contained only 9 per cent of this type of pupil' (p. 149). Where teachers used a lot of class-directed activity there was less distraction and fewer intermittent workers. A large proportion of their classes were solitary workers who had little individual contact with their teachers.

Teachers who were group instructors were able to share their time more evenly among the pupils and had a higher ratio of quiet collaborators to attention seekers. The reverse was true of the infrequent changers who had the highest proportion of attention seekers.

The rotating changers and habitual changers had higher proportions of intermittent workers but fewer solitary workers.

The Oracle study also found that pupils spent more time in work activity in formal classrooms and more time in distraction or other activities in informal ones. Pupils in informal classrooms had 50 per cent less contact with the teacher than pupils in formal classrooms.

Developing a personal style

As a teacher you need to develop your own personal style and discover the best way of working in the classroom for you. This will depend on your strengths and limitations and, as we have seen, your personality, experience and philosophy. You have decisions to make about many of the things that will happen in the classroom. For example, you have to decide how far you will have children doing different activities at the same time and how far everyone should be engaged on the same topic. Mortimore *et al.* (1988: 230) found:

> There was some evidence that where pupils worked on the same task as other pupils of roughly the same ability, or when all the pupils worked on the same curriculum area but on different tasks at their own level, the effective upon progress was positive. In contrast, where all pupils worked exactly the same task the effects were negative.

They also found that a high degree of choice over work tended to result in poorer progress whereas a limited amount of choice gave positive results.

> When the pupils' day was given a structure or framework by the teacher such that children were given single tasks to undertake over fairly short periods of time such as a lesson or an afternoon, and were encouraged to manage the completion of the tasks independently of the teacher, the impact was positive for a range of cognitive and non-cognitive outcomes.
>
> (1988: 229)

Part of your style involves deciding how far to plan ahead and how far to play it by ear. Cortazzi (1991) in a study of the way 123 primary teachers worked, found that virtually all of them often departed from their pre-planned work to follow a direction which the children indicated. They often made use of things the children brought in or events which cropped up. This is less easy to do under the pressures of the National Curriculum but things will arise unexpectedly which will fit in with the demands of the National Curriculum. Cortazzi's teachers gave as their reasons for 'playing

it by ear' as 'First, *flexibility*, second, the *need for talk*, and third, most impor-
tantly, the need to follow the children's *enjoyment, excitement and interest*'
(p. 72). He found that the more experienced teachers were the more they
tended to play it by ear.

You will have a preference for the extent to which you teach the whole
class, the group and the individual. We have already seen from the Oracle
study that teachers who work with individuals a great deal of the time have
more children in their classes who waste time. Whole-class teaching can be
difficult to relate to the range of abilities in the class but if you are the kind
of teacher who can hold children's attention riveted when you wish, you
should make the most of it. Interactive whole-class teaching can also be effective when you discuss with the children the topic in hand. Group teaching
to some extent overcomes the problem of the range of abilities and allows
you to group by ability. Cooperative group work, which requires a different
kind of grouping, is also valuable. Good teachers use a range of methods but
the particular range you choose will reflect your personal style.

Another aspect of style is how far you use competition and how far you
emphasise cooperation. Children are naturally competitive and you don't
need to introduce competition to find them competing. Some children thrive
on a competitive atmosphere. Others are discouraged because they fail too
often. You need to keep a balance for competition and encourage children
to compete against their own previous performance. At the same time you
need to encourage cooperation which is a useful ability in life and needs
training in children. The researches suggest that there is comparatively little
cooperative working in classroom.

Mortimore *et al.* (1988: 241) found that:

> The teacher's attitude towards the class appeared to be particularly
> important for pupil's non-cognitive outcomes. Enthusiastic teachers
> provided their pupils with more stimulating activities, and made
> more use of higher-order communication; their work was better
> organised and, in turn, pupils were more interested in work; they
> praised pupils' work more often and also reported being more satis-
> fied with their job.

The teacher's tasks

Observation

As a teacher you must observe and listen to children in order to be able to
match the learning programme to individual needs. There is evidence that
teachers are not altogether successful at this. The Primary Survey (DES 1978)
found that teachers were better at matching work to children in language and
mathematics than in other subjects and many HMI reports have commented

that the most able were not extended. Bennett *et al.* (1984) found that teachers tended to underestimate the most able. Desforges and Cockburn (1987: 102) studied the mathematics work of a number of infant teachers and made the following observation: 'The teachers did not find out about the degree of match between the tasks and children's attainment because they did not conduct any detailed diagnostic work.' While it is not altogether surprising that teachers do not always manage to match work to children given the number of children a teacher deals with, it is something that needs to be kept in mind.

The teacher needs not only to observe and listen but also to interpret what is seen and heard. Bennett *et al.* (1984) found that teachers tended not to be sufficiently diagnostic in their conversations with children. This has probably improved since this research was done with the assessment demands of the National Curriculum. A more recent study by Askew *et al.* (1995: 94) found that the most effective teachers of mathematics 'carefully documented information about pupils' learning and then used it to inform and develop their teaching'. In contrast, less effective teachers simply used assessment to check what had been learned and 'any gaps in understanding were dealt with through re-teaching and practice' (p. 94).

Observing children may involve careful questioning to find out how they are thinking. Askew *et al.* note that 'Knowledgeable teachers questioned their pupils about problem-solving processes and listened to their responses, while the less knowledgeable teachers tended to explain problem-solving processes to pupils or just observe their pupils' solutions' (p. 20).

It is important not only to observe informally as part of the day-to-day work, but also to do some systematic observation, reviewing children's performance in turn over a period of time. Systematic observation may include the use of tests and check-lists.

Planning

Observing children and attempting to match their observed needs leads naturally to planning the provision of the learning and teaching programme. Teachers need to plan long term, medium term and short term. Suggestions for this are set out in the National Literacy Strategy (DfEE 1998a). Long-term plans cover the year, medium-term, the term or half-term and short-term, the week and the day. Planning needs to reflect long- and short-term aims and targets.

In planning teachers need to be clear about their aims for the curriculum in general and their objectives for the short term. Cooper and McIntyre (1996: 79) found that teachers had both cognitive and affective aims and that these could be in conflict.

> Prominent affective aims include engendering in pupils a sense of security and willingness to participate in class/group discussion, and

encouraging pupils to adopt a positive attitude to the subject area and to derive pleasure from study ... Cognitive aims related to pupils' acquisition of particular knowledge, their cognitive development, their understanding of concepts and their mastery of specific skills.

They also found that the coming of the National Curriculum had encouraged teachers to spend time discussing effective teaching methods with colleagues.

Long- and medium-term planning involves making broad outlines of curriculum plans and setting dates or periods of time for completing different aspects of the work or meeting specific targets. It also involves considering how you wish the children to work and planning any training necessary to implement this. Part of planning is considering how work will be evaluated and the records you will keep and this may involve building in ways of evaluating and recording which are economical of time. You also need to consider in advance the books, equipment and materials you will need and take any necessary action. Your plans should include, where appropriate, the provision of first-hand experience in the shape of visits or field studies, since these need to be planned well in advance. You may also need to consider whether you personally need to develop any knowledge, particular skills or expertise in connection with these plans.

Short-term planning involves defining short-term aims and objectives, thinking in detail about how you will actually present work, the questions you will ask, the way you will group children for learning, how you will provide for the different abilities within the class, what work the children will actually do to consolidate their learning and how you will record and evaluate the work done.

Consideration of planning needs to include consideration of continuity. This involves not only thought about how children beginning school have continuity between their home experience and their school experience and how continuity from year to year and teacher to teacher is managed, but continuity between one piece of work and the next, between one project and another and between subject areas. Webb and Vulliamy (1996: 78) also point out that when continuity from year to year is considered there are aspects of continuity which need consideration other than curriculum content:

- the degree to which pupils are encouraged to be independent;
- pupil participation in decision making;
- the use of pupil self-assessment;
- the range of teaching methods and resources used;
- the criteria and standards employed for the presentation and content of work;
- the expectation and approaches to assessment.

The organisation of the environment

Another task of the teacher is the organisation of the learning environment. This means considering how you want children to be seated, how you will arrange materials so that children can find what they need without constant reference to you, the use of display and your plans for keeping the environment orderly.

Assessment and recording

A very important part of the teacher's task is that of assessing and recording children's progress and development. This has become much more important with the development of the assessment programme for the National Curriculum. Gipps *et al.* (1995: 23) studied the effect on teachers of the requirement to assess children as part of the testing at Key Stages 1 and 2. They found that:

> In 1991 many of our Year 2 teachers, in preparation for teacher assessment, began to do three things:
>
> - collect evidence of children's work which they would then save as proof, including such things as photographs (especially in science) and tape recordings of reading;
> - use observation (especially in mathematics and science) as a technique of assessment;
> - record the information.

In particular some teachers took detailed notes of their observations, questioned children closely to determine understanding, and planned assessment into their teaching.

The knowledge and skills teachers need

In the first instance, a teacher needs self-knowledge. Only when you know yourself and recognise your own strengths and weaknesses can you work effectively, making the most of the things you do well and finding ways of overcoming or compensating for your shortcomings.

Webb and Vulliamy (1996) suggest that teachers need subject knowledge which 'includes not only the basic concepts and procedures of the discipline but also the pedagogical content knowledge which includes ways of representing the subject to others through explanations, analogies, illustrations, examples and demonstrations' (p. 60).

Bennett *et al.* (1992) studied the extent to which teachers perceived themselves to be competent in the subjects of the National Curriculum. They found that teachers felt most competent in mathematics and English. Science ranked third. Technology ranked tenth and in Webb and Vulliamy's study it was also the subject causing the greatest difficulty.

As a teacher you need to know about children. You need to know how they learn and what motivates them both collectively and individually. You need specific information about each child. You need to know something of his or her background and his or her personality and learning style, how best each child learns. You need to be aware of the kinds of experiences your children have so that you can match your teaching to them. You also need to know the stage of development each child has reached and his or her particular abilities.

Children have a much greater power for learning than we often manage to tap in classrooms. They have already mastered an immense intellectual task in learning to speak and they managed this without being taught in the sense that teachers attempt to teach them in school. Some children also possess a considerable knowledge of hobbies and other interests. Most people are motivated by problems within their capacity and the more you can present learning as an interesting challenge the more your children are likely to learn.

Baird (1992) studied the lessons of a number of teachers and discussed them with the teachers and the pupils. He found that some teachers gave insufficient attention to the affective side of learning, for example the need to be stimulating, inspiring, challenging, perceptive, concentrating instead on the cognitive side. He concluded that only when teachers had these two aspects of children's learning in balance were pupils really interested and ready to learn. This work was done in secondary schools and primary teachers are more likely to keep these two aspects of their work in harmony because of the nature of young children, but it is worth considering if children appear to be uninterested in work whether there is enough emphasis on the affective side.

Praise and reward are more effective motivators than criticism. You need to use praise very specifically for behaviour that you want to reinforce. Mortimore *et al.* (1988: 85) found that 'Positive feedback, in the form of praise about work, was observed very infrequently.' They also found that the use of praise decreased as children grew older and feedback about work tended to be neutral. Teachers also tend to use praise for work more frequently than for behaviour.

Learning involves using the material learned as soon as possible. Using learning can involve talking about it. You need to consider with any new piece of learning how children can put it to use or talk about it. Group or class discussion may be useful.

We understand the words of others if we can draw on our own experience to interpret them. This is particularly important with children, whose experience of the world is more limited than that of adults. You may assume that children have experience of something because you experienced it as a child but the children's experience may be different from yours. Children may also use words with apparent understanding but have only a limited knowledge of the full meaning. You can never take their understanding for granted and you often need to question it.

Children also need to be helped to structure their learning so that it is accessible when they need it. Structuring means classifying what is being learned in a way that helps children to add new learning to what they already know. You can help with this process by teaching in a structured way and suggesting ways in which children can remember things through association and classification.

A teacher needs to know how to organise and control work in the class-room. This is considered in detail in Chapter 7. Organisation involves creating a learning environment which is not only attractive and welcoming but also well-organised for work, so that children can easily obtain what they need and return it when they have finished with it.

Organising work also involves considering how to group children for different aspects of the curriculum. This is particularly important for children with special needs and for the very able, but there should also be work where children have to cooperate and work together. This is dealt with in Chapter 8.

The best organisation of the classroom environment will not work if you are not in control of the children. Children need training in using the environment and in working in the ways you want.

Teachers also need to be good at problem-solving. In some senses teaching is all about solving a succession of problems. How best to explain some-thing to the class? How to teach Johnny to do subtraction? How to persuade Mary to concentrate on her work instead of chatting to her next door neigh-bour? Children also need to learn problem-solving skills, particularly in science and technology and techniques which work for you can also work for them.

It helps to start by defining the problem. This serves to clear your mind and identify what the problem really is. For example, your problem may be the behaviour of a particular boy in the class who finds it difficult to concentrate on work and spends his time disturbing other people.

It then helps to define the problem further by making some statements about it. For example, you might make statements such as the following:

- Lee rarely finishes his work because he finds it difficult to concentrate.
- Other people sitting near Lee find it difficult to concentrate on their work because he keeps disturbing them.

The next step is to define your objectives. In this case it would be to help Lee to concentrate and work without disturbing others. When you are clear about the nature of the problem it then becomes possible to consider a range of solutions. One would be to sit Lee apart from other children perhaps in a space made by moving a cupboard or bookcase at right angles to the wall so that he is not looking at what other people are doing. It may help if he sits facing the wall rather than the rest of the classroom.

A useful way of working in this situation is to use some form of behaviour modification. This would involve in the first instance collecting evidence of the number of times Lee apparently stops work or disturbs others and discussing this with him, suggesting that he aims to reduce this number. You might then give him the goal of working for ten minutes by the clock without stopping work or talking to anyone else. If he succeeds in doing this his behaviour should be reinforced by some form of reward. This may be simply praise for success or he can keep a record of the number of times he can work for ten minutes without stopping. When he has done this a given number of times he can move to do something he particularly enjoys. The length of time he works can be decreased if it appears to be too long or increased as he gradually becomes more able to work. It is important that you notice and praise him when he succeeds each time. This is not easy in a busy classroom but it can be done.

Wheldall and Merrett (1984) in describing behaviour modification in the classroom also suggest that teachers sometimes reinforce bad behaviour by giving it too much attention. The child in question may be seeking attention and find that misbehaving is one way to attract it. It is not easy to ignore misbehaviour because of the spin-off effect on other children but the idea is to reinforce the positive behaviour all the time so that the child gets your attention by behaving well.

Teachers need good communication skills. These involve skills in presentation and explanation, skill in questioning and leading discussion as well as skill in listening to children and interpreting what they say so that you can diagnose the problems which are holding up their learning.

Reflective teaching

Stoll and Fink (1996: 118) state that 'Reflection is the process or art of analysing one's actions, decisions or products by focusing on the process of achieving them.'

Teachers need to be constantly reflecting on their work, looking at their aims in relation to the outcomes, being open-minded about children's potential and making judgements about whether the activities of a particular lesson or series of lessons were the best possible ways of helping children to learn. Reflection should lead to action.

Pollard and Tann (1987: 5) define a reflective teacher as 'one who constantly questions his or her own aims and actions, monitors practice and outcomes, and considers the short-term and long-term effects upon each child'. They also say 'We all have strengths and weaknesses and most teachers would agree that classroom life tends to reveal these fairly quickly. Reflective teaching is, therefore, a great deal to do with facing such features of ourselves in a constructive manner and in a way which incorporates a continuous capacity to change and develop' (p. 18).

They describe reflective teaching as follows:

- Reflective teaching implies an active concern with aims and consequences, as well as with means and technical efficiency.
- Reflective teaching combines enquiry and implementation skills with attitudes of open-mindedness, responsibility and wholeheartedness.
- Reflective teaching is applied in a cyclical or spiralling process in which teachers continually monitor, evaluate and revise their own practice.
- Reflective teaching is based on teacher judgement, informed partly by self-reflection and partly by insights from educational disciplines.

(Pollard and Tann 1987: 1)

Cooper and McIntyre (1996: 76) suggest that 'Professional craft knowledge is the knowledge that teachers develop through the processes of reflection and practical problem-solving that they engage in to carry out the demands of their jobs.' They go on to say that the problem is 'that because teachers have so little time for reflection there is often too little opportunity for the kind of exploration that the uncovering of craft knowledge requires'. Their study found that 'teachers place a high value on the opportunity to artic-ulate such knowledge and it is suggested that the process of articulation enables teachers to obtain deeper understanding of their own practice than would be possible without such articulation' (p. 76).

We have already noted that teachers need to be skilled at observing children and interpreting what they see and what they find out from ques-tioning. Teachers need to be good at diagnosis and the research evidence is that they find this very difficult, partly because of the pressures on them in the classroom. Teachers need to be skilled at organising work in the classroom and controlling the situation. The classroom needs to be a learning environment.

Wragg (1993: 15) studied children's views of teachers and found that they tended to prefer teachers who:

- are slightly strict, but not over-severe or permissive
- are fair in their use of rewards and punishments
- treat them as individuals
- are interesting and provide a variety of stimulating work

- are friendly and good-humoured, but not sarcastic
- explain things clearly

Stress

A great deal has been said recently about the effect of stress on teachers and there have been many pressures which have helped to create stress. Kyriacou (1991: 137) suggests that the following are causes of stress:

- pupils with poor attitudes and motivation towards their work;
- pupils who misbehave and general class indiscipline;
- rapid changes in curriculum and organisational demands;
- poor working conditions, including career prospects, facilities and resources;
- time pressures;
- conflicts with colleagues;
- feeling undervalued by society.

He points out that 'the experience of stress is triggered by the perception of threat to your self-esteem or well-being' (p. 137). Stress may make you disaffected with teaching and may undermine your relationship with pupils and the way you react to problems and difficulties. He goes on to say

You need to identify what is causing you stress and why and then decide on a course of action that will deal successfully with that cause of stress. . . . Particularly useful are mental techniques such as getting things in perspective, trying to see the humour in a situation, trying to detach yourself from personal and emotional involvement in a situation, and sharing your worries and concerns with others.

(Kyriacou 1991: 138)

5

THE CLASSROOM CLIMATE

If effective learning is to take place, the classroom climate needs to be supportive, unthreatening, encouraging and sensitive to individuals. Children need to feel confident so that they can risk getting something wrong. As the teacher you need to be friendly to all children, yet sufficiently detached to be able to be objective about identifying children's needs. You need to be kind but firm and consistent in dealing with everyone in the class and teacher/pupil relationships need to be based on mutual respect.

Pollard and Tann (1987) quote Carl Rogers (1961) who suggested that there are three basic qualities required for a warm person-centred relationship. These are acceptance, genuineness and empathy. Pollard and Tann suggest that 'acceptance involves acknowledging and receiving children "as they are"; genuineness implies that such acceptance is real and heartfelt; while empathy suggests that a teacher is able to appreciate what classroom events feel like to children' (p. 64).

There is a tension between teacher and children which is an inevitable result of the difference in their positions. Pollard (1985: 159) describes the teacher as watching the children, 'interpreting their actions from the point of view of her perspective and evaluating the effect of them on her interests'. The children 'watch and evaluate, gradually accumulating a stock of knowledge and experience of the teacher, most of which is organised around the threat of teacher power'.

Kyriacou (1986: 6) notes that: 'At the heart of effective teaching must be the ability of the teacher to create the right emotional climate and tone for the lesson, which will enable pupils to engage appropriately in the mental attitude required for learning to take place satisfactorily.' He also states that: 'An effective classroom climate is one in which the teacher's authority to organise and manage the learning activities is accepted by the pupils, there is mutual respect and good rapport, and the atmosphere is one of purposefulness and confidence in learning' (p. 143).

Galloway (1990: 221) stresses the following:

The nature and quality of social interaction will reflect the ethos or moral climate of the class. The moral climate refers to the climate of social expectations that influence relationships between pupils, between a teacher and pupils and, outside the classroom, between teachers. It is also reflected in the teacher's order of priorities and in the value ascribed to the achievement of particular pupils or a group of pupils.

Cooper and McIntyre (1996: 155), describing a study of effective teaching and learning, make the following points about the social climate of the classroom: 'The social climate of the classroom, particularly in relation to the ways in which teachers related to pupils, was a significant factor for pupils, determining, in some cases, the degree to which they employed their most effective strategies or whether they chose to employ them at all.'

Classroom rules

When children first come to school, whether in infant classes or nursery school, they have to learn the role of pupil. Edwards and Knight (1994: 14) suggest that 'One of the difficulties that early years practitioners have to manage is the need to maintain children's sense of personal effectiveness while they are learning to operate in a context in which the social rules and amount of adult attention will be very different [from home].' They go on to describe the way in which reception class teachers act as if children already know the rules and routines of the classroom praising those who conform to them.

Teachers generally establish classroom rules either by stating them explicitly or by the way they react to the way children behave. Pollard (1985: 161) suggests that rules, 'develop through incident and case law as the teacher and children come to understand each other and to define the parameters of acceptable behaviour in particular situations'. Over time the children learn to conform to these rules and you need to be ready to discuss and negotiate them where necessary. Children will test out the rules which you seem to be putting forward to see how far they can go.

Docking (1992: 27) suggests that classroom rules serve three overlapping purposes:

- to ensure safety and personal welfare;
- to provide effective conditions for teaching and learning;
- to help children develop considerate behaviour and respect for property.

He notes that rules often cover the following issues:

- entering, leaving and moving around the room;
- handling materials and equipment;
- talking and listening;
- treating others as you would like them to treat you;
- making the room a pleasanter place to be in.

He makes the point that 'Constructive relations with the children are more likely to be promoted if the rules are generally phrased in terms of the behaviour wanted rather than the behaviour not wanted' (p. 28).

Wragg (1993: 31) makes the point that 'learning takes place where positive relationships exist between a teacher and the class and amongst pupils. The teacher's role is to develop a healthy classroom climate within which learning will automatically thrive.'

It is also wise to discuss possible rules with children and give them the opportunity to suggest rules themselves so that they feel some ownership of them.

Rules need to be introduced gradually and some of them will be deduced by the children from your behaviour. This is one of the problems that children encounter when they start school – they need to learn how to behave in the classroom. They may also need to learn how to relate to and interact with their peer group and although most children now have some pre-school experience which makes this rather easier, there is still much learning needed.

Expectation and reinforcement

An important part of the climate of the classroom is the way you offer positive reinforcement to children giving them praise for behaviour as well as for achievement and for effort. It is helpful if teachers of young children, in particular, make a point of praising children for exercising social skills. It may also be a good idea to discuss social behaviour quite frequently so that children gradually come to recognise what is required of them and how they can learn to get on with others. Some children appear to have social skills quite naturally or to have acquired them easily in pre-school or at home. Others need help in their acquisition.

Teacher expectation is an important factor in children's achievement and you need to be constantly conveying the idea that much is expected of children. There is a famous study by Rosenthal and Jacobson (1968) in which teachers were deliberately misled about the potential of their pupils so that they were told that some were more able than others. Later testing showed that the pupils who had been incorrectly designated as more able actually showed higher test results. This study suggests that the teachers in question treated the children who were said to be more able differently from other children and in doing this raised their level of performance. The study has been criticised on design grounds and attempts to replicate the study have not always been successful but the overall finding remains important for teachers.

Moyles (1992: 71) writes of study by Nash (1973) of primary teachers in Scotland:

> when it was found that the profile of particular children's performance in class varied considerably according to the teacher's manifested perception of them. Children favourably perceived by the teacher did well and said they liked being with that teacher, but where children did not do well, they were not favourably perceived by the teacher and reported not to like that teacher.

The problem for teachers about expectation is that your expectation of what children can achieve is the outcome of your experience. If you have consistently found that children of Caribbean origin, for example, tend to perform at a level below that of white children, or that working-class children appear to learn less well than children with a middle-class background, it is difficult for you to maintain high expectations of these groups of children. This leads to consideration of the problem of stereotyping. Teachers can easily assume that all children with a working-class background, or with local accents, are less intelligent than their peers. This leads them to treat these children as if this were the case and the children respond by behaving as if it were. The study of London schools by Mortimore *et al.* (1988) quoted in Chapter 3, which found teachers rating children from working-class backgrounds as less able than test results showed they actually were is a warning to teachers not to stereotype children but to be aware of how easy this is to do.

Typing individuals is something everyone does all the time. It is part of social interaction and is necessary for teachers if they are to cope with the complexity of the classroom and the immense variety that any group of children represents. The important thing is to be aware that one does it and that it can affect the way one treats people.

Tizard *et al.* (1988) found evidence that teachers tended to have lower expectations of children with non-standard English and lower verbal skills, lower social class background and problem behaviour, and higher expectations of children who were a pleasure to teach. They also found that teachers misclassified upwards the children who were a pleasure to teach and children with lower verbal skills were misclassified downwards. Some teachers also said that some curricular items were too difficult for their children although they were taught successfully in schools which were similar.

Cooper and McIntyre (1996: 143) found some indication that teachers tended to be rigid in typing children. 'It was indicated that teachers were resistant to changes in pupil behaviour that might undermine the identity that had been attributed.'

Alexander *et al.* (1992: 27) suggest that 'The mounting evidence about teacher under-expectation and pupil under-achievement means ... that teachers must avoid the pitfall of assuming that pupils' ability is fixed.'

Mortimore *et al.* (1988: 287) note that 'Teachers' expectations are transmitted in both direct and subtle ways. ... Where they differ for groups of pupils – girls rather than boys; children from middle-class families rather than from working-class; black rather than white ... they are perpetuating differences in achievement that are deeply unjust.'

Sammons *et al.* (1995: 17) state that 'if teachers set high standards for their pupils, let them know that they are expected to meet them, and provide intellectually challenging lessons to correspond to these expectations, then the impact on achievement can be considerable'. They go on to say 'Low expectations go hand-in-hand with a sense of lack of control over a pupil's difficulties and a passive approach to teaching. High expectations correspond to a more active role for teachers in helping pupils to learn' (p. 18).

Docking (1992: 76) suggests that 'the risk of generating low expectations of learning and behavioural potential might be reduced if teachers are determined to look for evidence which refutes negative labels which pupils have acquired'.

Expectation is particularly a matter for concern where pupils are grouped by ability. It is very easy to convey to less-able groups that they are not expected to achieve very much. On the other hand, in classes where there is no ability grouping, there is a danger of expecting too little from the most able children. You can only avoid these dangers by being aware of them and continually reflecting on your own practice, looking for occasions when you are subconsciously conveying views about the expectations of different children. Brophy and Good (1970), for example, found that teachers gave high-achievers a greater amount of praise following a correct answer and a smaller amount of criticism than other children. They also gave a greater number of repetitions or re-phrasings and clues following a wrong answer.

Alexander (1984: 43) sums up the dilemma teachers have in making judgements about children as follows:

> The more we come to know about children, about teaching and learning, and about the immense diversity and openness of knowledge, the more we have to accept that our best judgement of what a child can do, good though it is, is an approximation – not an absolute judgement but the most reliable and impartial which circumstances and our experience, knowledge and skills allow.

The hidden curriculum

Part of the classroom climate is the hidden curriculum – the things children are learning which are not made explicit. Alongside the official curriculum is another area of learning some of which is inferred from the behaviour of the teacher. If you appear to give greater value to the contribution of some children compared with others, this will be picked up by all the children who may demonstrate that they too value some children more than others. They will infer from your behaviour that some parts of the official curriculum are more important than others, that some behaviour is acceptable and some unacceptable and so on. All of this contributes to the overall classroom climate and you need to be very conscious of how quite small pieces of behaviour on your part will be interpreted by children.

There is a sense in which once an inference is made about behaviour, it is no longer hidden. It is part of an inferred curriculum. There will always be aspects which remain hidden, aspects of which the teacher is unaware. For example, do able children learn that it does not pay to work quickly because they will be given more work of a similar kind to do? Do some children spend time guessing the answer you want rather than trying to reason through to find the right answer? Do girls feel inferior to boys or vice versa? Do children get the impression that it is better to be white than black?

Desforges and Cockburn (1987: 37) studied the teaching of mathematics in the classes of a number of infant teachers and make the comment 'Many children were very anxious to please and, as a consequence, were more preoccupied with identifying the procedure which made the teacher happy rather than thinking about what they were doing.'

The inferred curriculum is important in keeping order and control in the classroom. The way that you signal the behaviour you want affects the way children behave. Galloway (1990: 216) notes that 'If the hidden curriculum fosters a climate in which all children expect, and are expected, to contribute to the work of the class, then the need for programmes focusing explicitly on the social development of individual children is greatly reduced.'

Eggleston (1992: 41) makes the following statement about the hidden curriculum: 'For most adults most of the official curriculum is ephemeral, soon to be forgotten in all but the most generalised recollection. But the learnings of the hidden curriculum endure, for they constitute the rules of living with one's fellows.'

He has a more limited definition of the hidden curriculum and defines its components as follows:

1   'Learning to live in crowds'.
2   'Learning to accept assessment by others, not only by the teacher but also by fellow pupils'.

3 'Learning how to compete to please both teachers and fellow students and obtain their praise, reward and esteem by appropriate behaviours'.
4 'Learning how to be differentiated'.
5 'Learning ways to control the speed and progress of what the teacher presents in the official curriculum'.

(Eggleston 1992: 37–39)

Edwards and Mercer (1987) noted that children, while not being aware of some of the rules of classroom behaviour, nevertheless accepted that the teacher controlled the discourse in the classroom, defining what it was appropriate to talk about and acting as arbiter of valid knowledge. The teacher's test questions needed to be answered with a degree of explicitness not needed in ordinary conversation. The repetition of a question implied that the answer given in the first place was wrong.

Personal and social education

Primary schools tend to take personal and social education for granted. Primary school teachers are almost all class teachers who see it as their responsibility to educate the whole child. One consequence of this is that not much thought is given to what should constitute the personal and social education programme.

Pathways to Life the Berkshire County Council (1997: 5) paper on personal and social education lists the following aims. They believe schools should encourage pupils to:

● Develop a balanced sense of worth, self-esteem and self-awareness and the confidence to be self-critical.
● Learn and apply appropriate behaviour in a range of situations and circumstances.
● Develop confidence and sensitivity in co-operating, negotiating, seeing things from more than one point of view and resolving conflict.
● Gain satisfaction and enjoyment from being contributing members of the school and the wider community.
● Develop adaptability, flexibility and the ability to exercise initiative.
● Develop an increasing awareness of and responsibility towards the immediate and wider environment.
● Take increasing responsibility for their own learning.

Lang (1988: 88) interviewed forty primary headteachers and teachers and found that they believed that:

- personal and social education was important;
- it didn't require any particular thought because of the special nature of primary schools;
- it was 'caught' not 'taught'.

He found that this view while widely held by primary schools did not always match the actual practice. A questionnaire to fifty-three heads and teachers from primary and middle schools demonstrated a tendency to feel that personal and social education was satisfactorily catered for. 'Replies to the question which asked how teachers helped children with problems suggested a much greater reliance on cure than prevention and what might be described as acts of faith rather than planned strategies' (p. 93). He found similar results when asking teachers how they helped children to get on with one another. 'Systematic consideration of school ethos and hidden curriculum did not often happen' (p. 93).

This area of work really needs to be considered at a whole school level but the actual implementation of a personal and social education programme has to take place in the classroom. All teachers, but particularly those who work with the youngest children, need to be concerned with socialisation, with helping children to learn to live in a community and get on with other children and adults. Next, teachers need to consider the development of each child as a growing person who is developing his or her self-image and self-esteem. This leads on to a consideration of relationships and the development of values and attitudes. The Berkshire County Council paper on personal and social education (1997: 6) suggests that schools need to consider and evaluate for pupils:

> Personal qualities and capabilities e.g. an awareness of personal strengths and weaknesses, an increased understanding of their emotional, social and physical development; an increased understanding of other people's responses and feelings, an acquisition of confidence and an ability to express their own personal opinions whilst respecting the views of others.

Lang (1990) suggests that while it is important that pastoral care has a proper place in the curriculum with an agreed structure and programme, much might also be done in the context of other work. The school needs to cater for the affective needs of children as well as their academic needs. He suggests that the school might use the following as a starting point for discussion, considering how each item might best be developed:

- Self-esteem: self-acceptance and a healthy self-image
- Self-confidence
- Personal and social skills

- Responsibility
- Initiative: the ability to undertake and sustain independent effort
- Honesty/trust: the ability to express feelings honestly and openly to others
- Empathy
- Judgement: the ability to make appropriate decisions independently and to adapt behaviour to the demands of the situation.

(Lang 1990: 102)

He goes on to suggest that 'a pastoral approach in the classroom would involve encouraging pupils both individually and in groups to think about and examine various aspects of their own development in order to gain a better understanding of themselves and others' (p. 103).

Maxwell (1990: 184) notes that 'through their experiences with friends, children learn to manage social relationships, understand and accommodate the feelings and actions of others, and relate to social rules and routines'. He goes on to say:

> If one of the main aims of school is to encourage the development of pupils into well-adjusted, socially competent adults, then the social life of the classroom has to be given consideration by the teacher. Consideration should include fostering appropriate relationships within the group and facilitating constructive group activity between friends, and the rooting of educational experiences designed to promote social or moral understanding in the context of children's day-to-day experience with their own friends.
>
> (Maxwell 1990: 184)

Citizenship is an area which is much under discussion at the present time and should be part of the curriculum. Health education, including sex education is also an important part of children's learning.

Braddy (1988: 161) gives the following aims for social learning:

- to encourage cooperation, sharing, caring;
- to encourage mutual respect;
- to encourage children to listen to each other;
- to encourage children to be friendly to each other and welcoming to newcomers;
- to help children to appreciate and accept differences between each other – sex, race, creed.

This is all part of the climate of the classroom and children will learn to behave in social ways with encouragement from the teacher. It is also part of the general climate of the school and may be reflected in the school's behaviour policy.

The way you react to children and to their work helps to shape their self-images. The way you deal with misbehaviour is also important. There should be an emphasis on thinking through what has happened and working out what would have been a better way to behave.

Whitaker (1988: 51) studied classroom activities in 550 primary and secondary schools and as a result of this study found that three teacher behaviours were especially significant:

- The teacher's ability to understand the meaning that classroom experience is having for each pupil.
- The respect and positive regard that the teacher has for each pupil as a separate person.
- The ability of the teacher to engage in genuine person-to-person relationship with each pupil.

He found that pupils in classes with teachers who demonstrated these qualities to a high degree made significantly greater gains in learning. They:

- became more adept at using higher cognitive processes such as problem-solving;
- had a higher self-concept;
- exercised greater learning initiatives in the classroom;
- exhibited fewer discipline problems;
- had a lower absence rate.

(Whitaker 1988: 53, 54)

As a teacher you may have in your class children who are coping with home problems such as family break up, bereavement, step-parent relationships, illness of parents or siblings, or parents who are themselves having difficulties such as unemployment which reflect on the children. For some, school may be a place of calm in a troubled world. It often helps such children to be able to talk to a sympathetic adult and it is important that they know that you know and sympathise with their difficulties. They may use opportunities to write in a personal way to express some of their feelings. Younger children may also try to express their feelings in painting or through play. Your attitude towards such children may encourage other children to be sympathetic also.

Charlton (1988: 65) writes of the need for teachers to be counsellors from time to time:

Occasions when children are being bullied by (or are bullying) peers, are upset by family bereavement, worried about aspects of their academic work, anxious about pending transfer to secondary school or concerned about the onset of puberty, represent a few of the personal social and academic problems and concerns which may well be alleviated by the efficient use of individual or group counselling skills by teachers in their classrooms.

He goes on to suggest that counselling may be used:

1   In a reaction sense responding to pupils' problems.
2   Integrated into teaching.
3   Proactively – 'to promote some aspect of the children's personal and social well-being'.

(Charlton 1988: 66).

Counselling involves listening to the other person carefully and trying to lead them to think through their problems. It does not involve trying to solve their problems yourself, though you may have suggestions to offer.

Bullying

Primary schools often tend to think that bullying is something that only happens in secondary schools. The evidence is that quite a number of children are subjected to bullying by their peers or by older children in the primary school. Besag (1989: 49) found that the headteacher of one school where parents and children felt that there was a serious problem, when asked about bullying replied, 'There is no problem here, the parents and children are over-reacting.'

She suggests that 'The most obvious reason for the lack of information about bullying is that children themselves will not discuss the difficulties they encounter with bullies.' She goes on to say 'In addition, the victims may feel so ashamed and degraded by the attacks and insults that they are quite unable to admit to this social failure' (p. 6). Elliott (1988) 'found that of those children who approached the teacher for help only 60 per cent of primary children and 40 per cent of older children considered that adults were either willing or able to alleviate their distress' (quoted by Besag 1989: 6).

Olweus (1993) studied bullying in schools in Norway and Sweden surveying large samples of children. He found that 15 per cent of children in primary and junior high schools in Norway were involved in bullying either as victims or as bullies. He found that the percentage of children who were bullied decreased as they grew older and it was the younger and weaker children who reported being the most exposed. He also found that 'bully/victim problems in primary schools were considerably more marked than previously assumed' (p. 16). There is no reason to suppose that the situation is any different in the United Kingdom. Besag found that bullies tended to be particularly active in the last year of both primary and secondary school and their victims were often younger children. She also found that seven out of ten bullies had strong racist attitudes.

All schools need to be on the alert for bullying and teachers need to be aware that it can go unnoticed if they are not vigilant. The child who wants to stay in at playtime or who seems to be alone in the playground or is comparatively friendless may be one who is suffering. Such a child may also be physically smaller and weaker than contemporaries. There may also be racist bullying. The fact that young children are usually fairly ready to complain about treatment by other children should not be allowed to disguise the fact that some children may be being bullied and are keeping quiet about it. It can be salutary to give older children a questionnaire which includes the question 'Have you ever been bullied?'

What should the teacher do about bullying if it is uncovered? Generally speaking punishment is not very effective and there is always the danger that the bully will take it out on a victim who reports what is happening to the teacher. One way of dealing with the problem is to try to help the bully to see the point of view of the victim. Bringing the bully and victim together, perhaps in a small group, may help, perhaps asking the group to suggest ways in which they could help the victim to have a happier time at playtime or after school or whenever the bully tended to operate.

It is also necessary to consider how to treat the victim of bullying. Besag (p. 58) suggests that:

> By keeping any intervention as far as possible impersonal, the confidence of the victim can more easily be restored. It is important to stress the normalcy of the situation, that it happens to most people at some time or other – even adults – and is a difficult situation to resolve alone, because the child may feel inadequate at being unable to cope.

Everything possible should be done to outlaw bullying. Ideally the school should have an anti-bullying policy. It should be discussed in the classroom and children encouraged to protect younger and more vulnerable children and to report bullying when they see it. Besag (p. 56) notes that 'Opportunity stimulates crime, so that sound supervision helps to prevent bullying because delinquent behaviour is not necessarily an innate characteristic of the individual, but occurs as a result of the interaction between the individual and the environment.'

Olweus suggests that classes should make rules about bullying. For example:

- We shall not bully other students.
- We shall try to help students who are bullied.

- We shall make a point to include students who become easily left out.

(Olweus 1993: 82)

Conclusions

The coming of the National Curriculum has brought both benefits and losses. Some teachers have found that while they are now offering a much broader curriculum than formerly, there is no longer time to pursue interesting topics which arise and themes which children have sparked off. This has made a change to a classroom climate in which it was possible to 'play it by ear' when something interesting occurred. It is nevertheless a tribute to creative teachers that so many have managed to still maintain a climate which values creativity. Woods (1995: 2) makes the following comment about creative teachers:

> They are inevitably constrained by systems and structures externally determined, but creative teachers can, to some extent, affect the situation in which they work, applying their values to changing or modifying the circumstances and increasing the range of opportunities. They cannot do this without a large measure of commitment to the values they espouse, and strong motivation, and indeed, on occasion, inspiration, in seeing them implemented.

Lang (1990: 104) suggests that in order to create a positive climate in their classroom teachers should:

- clearly define specific and realistic expectations with the minimum number of rules simply stated in positive terms, and do so as early as possible in the school year before difficulties arise in the classroom;
- involve pupils, whatever their stage and age in formulating or modifying these rules;
- make sure they communicate in advance to pupils any change in behavioural routines or expectations;
- notice and encourage appropriate classroom behaviour;
- emphasise strengths rather than weaknesses, rewards rather than punishments, encouragement rather than correction;
- provide opportunities for ongoing successful experiences that will enhance the self-esteem of each pupil in the classroom;
- promote and encourage the development of social skills within the curriculum.

6

EFFECTIVE TEACHING AND LEARNING

Perrott (1982: 4) suggests that the following are observable indications of effective teaching:

1   Pupils show knowledge and understanding, skills and attitudes intended by the curriculum as measured by performance on tests.
2   Pupils exhibit independent behaviour in learning curriculum content.
3   Pupils exhibit behaviour which indicates a positive attitude towards teacher and peers.
4   Pupils exhibit behaviour which indicates a positive attitude towards the curriculum and the school.
5   Pupils exhibit behaviour which indicates a positive attitude towards themselves as learners.
6   Pupils do not exhibit behaviour problems in class.
7   Pupils seem actively engaged in learning academically relevant material while the class is in session.

In considering effective teaching and learning we need to look at the content of what we teach as well as the way in which we teach it. While much of what is currently taught in British schools is based on the National Curriculum, teachers also need to look more widely at what is needed for the future by today's children.

The National Curriculum set out to provide a broad and balanced curriculum for all children which would be a move away from the traditional emphasis on English and mathematics. The recent suggestion that schools should ensure that the core subjects are given priority rather than strive to teach the curriculum in all subjects may have made things easier for teachers but militates against the broad and balanced curriculum and schools need to try to ensure that in spite of the pressures on time other subjects get reasonable coverage. Campbell and Neill (1992), looking at the use of time in primary schools, found 56 per cent of time was given to the core subjects and only 30 per cent to the other foundation subjects and 12 per cent to assessment and SATs. Two per cent went on other teaching.

Pollard (1996b: 33) states that 'Children will filter and interpret what they are taught as they struggle to make sense of it, so that we cannot assume that what children learn is a direct reflection of the curriculum which is presented to them.'

The effectiveness of teaching depends also on the knowledge that teachers have of their subject. The National Curriculum has made new demands for knowledge in many areas and teachers have had to work hard to bring their own knowledge up to date. Webb and Vulliamy (1996) found that technology was the subject causing the greatest difficulty. They also found that one school using specialist teaching for history, geography, science and technology at Key Stage 2 found it valuable in enabling teachers to see progression in the work.

A great deal of research has looked at effective teaching and learning but effectiveness is still a very personal affair. A teacher can do all the things suggested by research and still not succeed, or go his or her own way and succeed very well. Effectiveness is not only a matter of working in accepted ways but also a matter of personality and personal style. Brophy and Good (1986: 329) quote Medley (1979) who suggested that there were five conceptions of the effective teacher:

a) possessor of desirable personal traits;
b) user of effective methods;
c) creator of a good classroom atmosphere;
d) master of a repertoire of competencies;
e) professional decision maker who has not only mastered needed competencies but learned when to apply them and how to orchestrate them.

Brophy and Good (1986: 341), in studying the work of effective teachers, also found that:

The teachers who produced the most achievement also assumed personal responsibility for doing so. Their interviews revealed feelings of efficacy and internal locus of control, a tendency to organise their classrooms and to plan activities proactively on a daily basis, and a 'can do' attitude about overcoming problems.

Galton (1995), on the other hand, found that many teachers did not accept responsibility for children's achievement in the full sense, attributing failure of pupils to learn to external factors such as the children's home background.

There is some evidence that we tend to underestimate the learning which children can achieve, given the right opportunities. Whitaker (1988: 39) states 'We have hugely underestimated the power of the brain and the capacity of the young to achieve far more than we ever thought possible.'

Moyles (1992: 32) lists the characteristics of effective teachers as found by research in Britain and the USA. She found that their classroom organisation and management included:

- creating a suitable atmosphere for learning which is positive and consistent;
- thorough planning and preparation of curricular frameworks and progression;
- using a variety of methods of whole class, group and individual teaching;
- systematic organisation of resources and materials;
- having a classroom organised for curriculum needs;
- having well-established classroom routines;
- varied presentation of tasks and activities;
- lively teaching personality;
- making efficient use of time;
- establishing high standards of presentation of self and classroom;
- animated and clear presentation of tasks with good pacing and flow;
- clarity of learning intentions and sharing these with children;
- giving helpful feedback to children on their learning and helping children to evaluate themselves as learners;
- encouraging children to be self-sufficient and learn for its instrinsic motivation;
- having high expectation of all children as regards both activities and behaviour;
- matching learning to children's needs and using observation and assessment to inform planning;
- synthesising and analysing teaching/learning theories and classroom practices;
- regular evaluation of teaching and learning environment.

First-hand experience

An area important for primary school work which has not been much dealt with by research is the role of first-hand experience. A person understands the words of others, whether spoken or written, in terms of his or her experience. Young children have very limited experience and it is a quite difficult task for the teacher to find out what their experience is and link into it. You will only make sense to children if they can match your words with their experience.

You also need to provide a good deal of first-hand experience, both taking children out and bringing things and possibly people into the classroom.

The Bullock Report (DES 1975: 47, para. 4.2) made the following statement about this matter:

> We represent to ourselves, the objects, people and events that make up our environment, and do so cumulatively, thus creating an inner representation of the world as we have encountered it. The accumulated representation is on the one hand a storehouse of past experience and on the other a body of expectations regarding what may yet happen to us. . . . We interpret what we perceive at any given moment by relating it to our body of past experiences, and respond to it in the light of that interpretation.

Romberg and Carpenter (1986), writing of mathematics teaching and learning make the point that young children at the early stages can only solve problems if they can work with physical objects. They need the first-hand experience of handling something. This is also true of most aspects of the curriculum at the early stages. History and geography mean only as much as the teacher can find in the children's experience. Stories must also link with experience if they are to be understood.

As children grow and develop and widen their experience they become more able to envisage other times and places and the experience of other people. You can help this development by encouraging children to make images of experience in their minds. When reading poems or stories you can suggest making pictures in the mind. Sometimes the pictures in the mind can lead to artwork.

Woods (1995: 100) quotes a primary school child commenting on an exploration which had involved visiting an archaeological site:

> Now that we've actually been out on the dig and found parts of old times for ourselves, we can actually picture in our minds what it would have been like and if we wanted to we could make a play of it, but if we're just looking at a book then it's not reality really. You can really imagine it like when you're there.

He goes on to note that 'such teaching encourages learning that engages the students' full attention and powers. It motivates, stimulates, excites, unlocks and opens. It fosters a genuine spirit of enquiry and discovery. It leads to students' ownership of knowledge, internalised and integrated within their own system of relevances' (p. 105).

Of course it is not possible to provide first-hand experience for many aspects of children's education but it is important to bear in mind the need for matching children's experience in introducing new work. We only understand new material in terms of the knowledge and experience we already have. Learning involves mental activity on the part of the learner in linking new learning with past knowledge and experience.

Gipps (1994) writes of the constructivist model of learning contrasting it with a 'transmission' model which makes the assumption that the teacher is the source of knowledge and transmits it to the child who is seen as an empty vessel, receiving knowledge. 'Constructivist models of learning assume that knowledge is built up by the child in the form of connected schemata; the child is seen as an agent in his own learning actively constructing knowledge' (p. 24). First-hand experience is an essential part of the constructivist model.

Children thus gradually develop a model of the world in their own minds and this is closely linked with their development of language. Sammons *et al.* (1994: 57) suggest that 'children do their learning, and their thinking, through language'. They describe children as 'active *theorisers* in that, through talk, they are continuously trying to make sense of the world and the people in it, searching for patterns and regularities, and using the "feedback" that they get from their conversational partners to test out and modify their hunches and hypotheses'.

First-hand experience gives rise to new language and children do their sorting out by thinking and talking about it. It is important that there are plenty of opportunities for talk in the classroom both with the teacher and with other children in small groups. First-hand experience is also a very good way of stimulating written language especially if there has been a lot of talk about it first.

Experiential learning

First-hand experience is a form of experiential learning but there are other ways in which children can be involved in a powerful experience. Kyriacou (1986: 75) defines experiential learning as follows:

> Experiential learning . . . involves providing pupils with an experience which will totally and powerfully immerse them in 'experiencing' the issue which is being explored, and will as a result influence both their cognitive understanding, and also their affective appreciation (involving feelings, values and attitudes).

Experiential learning includes role play, direct experience, use of video and film and drama. Kyriacou goes on to describe the role of the teacher in this context:

> In experiential learning the role of the teacher is to set up a learning experience which encourages the pupils to reflect upon their own feelings, ideas and values; the climate of the classroom during

de-briefing work needs to be supportive and enabling rather than intellectually prescriptive.

(Kyriacou 1986: 76)

Structuring learning

Sotto (1994: 110) suggests that if people's natural capacity to learn has not been impaired, it looks as if they learn when:

- they find that there is something they wish to learn;
- they are able to tackle this reasonably directly;
- the task offers instrinsic rewards;
- the task is sensible and manageable;
- they can formulate hunches, test them and see the result of their actions;
- they are able to see patterns (or gain them tacitly);
- they find themselves in a challenging but friendly and supportive atmosphere.

When we learn something new, we deal with it first in working memory. This has limited capacity and we need to store what we have learned in the long-term memory which has an almost infinite capacity. The problem is that it is not always easy to retrieve what is stored in the long-term memory and it is therefore important to structure it so that it is easy to retrieve. Kyriacou (1986) makes the point that retrieval appears to be dependent upon the strength of the initial storage and the existence of links which can be used to locate what is stored. Teachers need to help children to structure what they are learning so that they are able to recall it. Wood (1988) suggests that the knowledge a child gains is really a joint construction by the child and a more expert person.

Romberg and Carpenter (1986) suggest that children learning material that is simply a matter of recall can be helped to improve the amount they remember by grouping the material in some way. Children need to be taught to structure material so that they can remember it.

You also need to do some structuring for children. Building up diagrams on the board, suggesting ways of thinking about new learning, presenting work in a structured form, pointing out, suggesting and praising, will all help. Scheerens (1992: 83) suggests that structured teaching involves 'making clear what has to be learnt (formulating learning objectives), splitting teaching into manageable units for the pupils and offering these in a well considered sequence; much exercise material in which pupils make use of "hunches" and prompts; regular testing for progress, with immediate feedback of the results'. However, it is important not to make structuring *for* the children a substitute for teaching them *how* to structure work for themselves.

Sutton (1981: 5) stresses the need for learners to reformulate learning for themselves:

1   Knowledge reformulated by the learner for himself is

    a)   more easily recalled;

    b)   linked to other knowledge, and so is accessible from other points in his thought patterns;

    c)   more easily *used* in daily living, or when solving a problem in some other field of thought;

    d)   influential upon future perceptions, and an aid to further learning in the subject.

2   Knowledge that the learner does not reformulate is

    a)   more easily forgotten;

    b)   usually remembered only in situations like those in which it was learned;

    c)   not applied or used elsewehere.

3   Reformulation may be provoked by

    a)   small group discussion;

    b)   by any writing which is the pupil's own composition, as long as pupils and teachers *expect* such reformulation, and the relationships between them allow it and encourage it.

Children are helped to structure their learning when objectives are clearly stated in a form which enables teacher and child to know when they have been achieved.

Matching work to children

Part of the teacher's task in structuring learning lies in matching work appropriately to children collectively and individually. The Primary Survey (DES 1978) found that in almost half the classes observed high-attaining children were given mismatched work in mathematics, and in geography, history and science the proportion of mismatch rose to almost two-thirds. They found that teachers seriously underestimated the more able but were somewhat better with the less able, although even here they found a mismatch of work to children of as much as 25 per cent.

Desforges (1985: 102) took part in a study of the matching of work in infant classes and concluded that mismatching appears to be initiated and sustained by:

    a)   demanding concrete records of procedures rather than evidence of thought;

b)   rewarding effort to produce rather than effort to conceptu-
     alise;
c)   adopting management techniques which permit rapid responses
     to each child's immediate problems but leave the teacher igno-
     rant of the child's confusions or potential;
d)   teachers' inexperience with and lack of skill in diagnostic work
     and a taste for direct instruction, however informally put, rather
     than analysis.

Bennett *et al.* (1984: 24, 25) studied the work of primary school children
and the extent to which teachers succeeded in matching work appropriately
to individuals. They identified five types of classroom tasks:

- Incremental – this simply involved accretion.
- Restructuring – here the pupil was 'required to discover, invent
  or construct a new way of looking at problems'.
- Enrichment – this demanded 'the use of familiar knowledge,
  concepts and skills in unfamiliar contexts'.
- Practice – this was a matter of making the learning automatic.
- Revision.

They then analysed the tasks which children were given according to these
definitions and found that 25 per cent were incremental tasks, 7 per cent
were restructuring and enrichment tasks, 60 per cent were practice tasks
and 6 per cent were revision tasks.

   They analysed the extent to which work was adequately matched to individual children and found that teachers had a tendency to underestimate
high-attaining children. Twenty-five per cent of these were misdiagnosed
compared with 13 per cent of mid-attainers and 9 per cent of low-attainers.
They found that almost a quarter of the tasks intended to make incremental
demands actually made practice demands because the child was already
familiar with the ideas. Similarly, in number work one in six tasks intended
to introduce new work turned out to be a practice task.

   It may be that the stress on assessment in recent years will have improved
this situation in today's classrooms, but the study still gives cause for concern
and many HMI studies and inspections have found that able children are not
sufficiently stretched.

   Matching work to children is not easy in large classes. The study described
found that teachers did not give sufficient emphasis to diagnosis of children's difficulties. When a child made an error the teacher simply re-taught
rather than probing to discover the thinking which had led to the error in
the first place.

   Vygotsky (1978: 86) writes of 'the zone of proximal development'. By
this he means the distance a child can go with help from another person,

normally an adult but sometimes another child. He describes it as 'the distance between the actual developmental level as determined by independent problem solving and the level of potential development as determined through problem solving under adult guidance or in collaboration with more capable peers'. As teacher you need to be aware of how far each child can go on his or her own and then provide appropriate guidance. Vygotsky suggests that 'developmental processes do not coincide with learning processes. Rather, the developmental process lags behind the learning process; this sequence then results in zones of proximal development' (p. 90).

Pollard (1996b: 74) suggests that the teacher, after discussing work, draws back a little and is then available to support children. 'He or she can offer questions, information or resources, suggest new strategies or provide other forms of instruction. This is where the children are "scaffolded" across their appropriate "zone of proximal development".'

Motivation for learning

An important part of the teacher's role is to motivate children to learn. Young children want to please the adult and this in itself is motivating and a great responsibility for the teacher. You have to make sure that the efforts made to please you are the result of work which is worthwhile.

People generally are motivated by inner need. We need to give and receive love, gain recognition for our contributions to a group and experience responsibility. Children need the recognition of the teacher and their peers. Praise is important in motivating children but it must be carefully matched to the situation and not indiscriminate.

Motivation can be intrinsic or extrinsic. Intrinsic motivation is motivation which comes from within the child. He or she wants to learn and succeed because of interest in the work in hand and satisfaction from completing the task. Extrinsic motivation is motivation from outside the child – a desire to gain good marks or please the teacher or parents. Generally speaking intrinsic motivation is a more satisfactory form.

Sotto (1994: 38) notes that research findings suggest that reliance on extrinsic rewards for learning lead to more superficial learning. 'These findings suggest that, instead of worrying about "reinforcing" or "rewarding", teachers would be better advised to try to devise learning tasks which enable learners to gain instrinsic rewards.'

He goes on to suggest that:

- if a task is organised so that learners find it intrinsically rewarding, nobody needs to 'reward' (or 'motivate') anybody;
- one of the main characteristics of a learning task which offers an intrinsic reward is that learners are actively engaged in it;

- the more responsibility the learners have for their learning, the greater their intrinsic reward is likely to be.

(Sotto 1994: 39)

This is a counsel of perfection. There is bound to be some learning which children need to undertake which needs rewarding because it is not necessarily rewarding in itself. There will also be some children who need the rewards of praise and encouragement for much of their work. It should also be remembered that there is need for reinforcement for appropriate behaviour.

Children may be motivated by the classroom environment. Display which shows work from all children from time to time may be motivating. There may also be things on display which interest children and spark off new work.

Most people enjoy problems which are interesting and challenging but within their capacity to solve. This can be seen in the interest which crosswords and other puzzles generate and in TV programmes like 'Countdown'. Children can be challenged to solve problems of various kinds and are more likely to remember things that they have worked out for themselves. For example, a child who has worked out the spelling rule that the vowel before a single consonant is likely to be long will probably remember that rule and apply it whereas a child given the rule and told to learn it may not. This is not to suggest that children should find out everything for themselves but to stress the importance of creating situations in which children are led to solve problems. The problems need careful matching to the children.

Children are also motivated by competition. Even if, as teacher, you avoid placing children in competitive situations in order not to affect the self-esteem of the less able children, they will make comparisons themselves and have a good idea of how they perform relative to their peers, especially as they grow older. The trouble with competition is that children may place too much emphasis on winning or on getting the answer the teacher wants rather than on the learning required or on thinking things out for themselves. There is also the problem that some children will always be among the losers and this affects their self-esteem and willingness to get down to learning. Nevertheless, competition has its place, particularly where it is competition with yourself or with someone of comparable ability. All children need to learn to lose as well as to win. Boys, in particular, tend to thrive on competition.

Children may be motivated by having individual targets to aim for, aiming at self-improvement. They may also find cooperative activity motivating. There is a satisfaction in working as part of a group. Teaching someone else can also motivate. The child doing the teaching has to make sure of his or her own knowledge in order to act as teacher. Children can also often help each other by putting learning into words which the learner is likely to understand. Some schools have experimented with pairing classes

60

of different age groups and allowing children in the older class to teach the younger in a limited area. This can be a strong motivation for children in the older class who have to learn well and prepare themselves to teach the younger children. Writing books for the younger children to read may well motivate some good written work by the older children who have to study what will interest the younger children and put it into suitable language.

Computers and audio-visual equipment generally are motivating for children. Computers represent a very considerable learning resource for the future particularly when it becomes more widely possible to interact with the computer with the voice. Programs which really teach new work, analysing children's errors and correcting them, will create a new order in the classroom of the future.

The way an individual child attributes the causes of success or failure affects his or her motivation. Success or failure may be attributed to effort, to ability or luck. Young children tend to see effort as a major cause of success or failure. It is only later that ability comes to be seen as something which sets a limit on what can be achieved. This will be seen as a relatively stable cause for failure or success, whereas effort is more variable. Rogers (1990: 98a) makes the point that the individual who attributes success to high ability and failure to low effort finds that each success leads to higher expectation and failure has a less marked effect. 'Conversely, the individual who attributes success to high effort and failure to low ability will increasingly come to expect failure.' Continued failure leads to low self-esteem and gradually to opting out of the attempt to achieve.

Young children tend to attribute success to effort rather than ability and it is only towards the end of primary schooling that they come to see ability in a more adult way as something which is relatively stable. Rogers (1990b: 38) notes that 'A failure attributed to lack of effort is less threatening than one attributed to lack of ability, as the former attribution allows us to accept the fact of failure but refutes the allegation that it implies a lack of compentence on our part.'

He also suggests that:

> Competition is . . . likely to make children more concerned with adopting self-defensive strategies designed to protect them from the worst consequences of failure (the assumption that one lacks the necessary level of ability) and less likely to be mastery-oriented (concerned with gaining their best level of understanding of the requirements of the task in hand).
>
> (1990b: 37)

Another important element in motivation is feedback. Children need to know how they are doing as soon as possible and the feedback the teacher gives can motivate them to further effort. Kyriacou (1986: 50) suggests that 'helpful and supportive feedback is seen to be an important characteristic of effective teaching, while hostile and deprecating feedback is not'. He also suggests that feedback should be quick and constructive whether given collectively or individually. There is a need to establish the root of any problem – for example, 'initial inattentiveness, not being able to understand the task, a lack of interest in the topic, an application of a faulty learning strategy' (p. 124).

This is not to say that there should be no criticism. Galton (1989: 141) notes that 'this is a most difficult area because the teacher needs to be simultaneously supportive of what the child has achieved but also critical so that clear standards are set and agreed between all participants in the learning process.'

The right use of praise is also important. Teachers need to praise for very specific pieces of work or behaviour so that children are encouraged to repeat the experience. A statement such as 'I liked the way you started your story with a conversation' is better than a statement such as 'I liked your story' because it is more specific and addresses something you may want to encourage. Similarly with behaviour. Teachers generally praise work more often than behaviour.

Pollard and Tann (1987) suggest that teachers should analyse their written feedback to children from time to time reviewing what they have written under headings such as encouragement given, diagnostic advice given, extension proposed, no comment, discouragement given. This sounds a tall order if a teacher were to try and go back over work done in the past, but is a possible thing to do in the process of marking a piece of work.

Teaching methods

Teachers have to decide during every day and during every part of every day how they should teach something. You have to decide what should be learned by discovery and what should be taught directly, the place of discussion and questioning, the role of cooperative work and the place of individual work.

HMI (DES 1985a) suggested that teachers needed to consider four key elements in their thinking about the curriculum. These were knowledge, skills, concepts and attitudes. Pollard (1996b: 35) summarises these as follows:

- extend children's *knowledge* in their area of study;
- develop *skills* which enable children to control and direct their own learning, including social, linguistic, scientific, mathematical and manipulative skills;
- build *concepts* which enable children to organise, generalise and relate ideas and thus form a basis for analysis and for making informed judgements;

- develop positive *attitudes* in the children towards both learning and each other. For instance, to question, to listen, to observe, to concentrate when learning. To respect each other and the cultures which make up our society, to work both individually and cooperatively with others.

Direct teaching

Direct teaching whether to the whole class or to a group may be the most efficient and economical way of getting children to learn something and checking that they know it. It is particularly useful as a starting point for new work and as a summing up process at the end of a piece of work. A good teacher can do much to stimulate interest and can be inspirational in dealing with the class or group. It can also be a good way of dealing with issues of safety or organisation where it is important that every child understands the same thing.

We have heard a good deal in recent months about interactive whole-class teaching in which the teacher involves individual children while maintaining the attention of the whole class. This is particularly useful in number work where individuals can be involved in answering different parts of problems the whole class is discussing.

Kyriacou (1986) suggests that teachers need to think about the kind of educational outcomes that they are trying to foster. These might be facts, concepts, intellectual skills, problem-solving strategies, transfer of learning, attitudes, general learning skills or consolidation of previous learning. He suggests that there are three main uses for teacher exposition:

1   making clear the structure and purpose of the learning experience;
2   informing, describing and explaining;
3   using questions and discussion to facilitate and explore pupils' learning.

(Kyriacou 1986: 57)

Wragg and Brown (1993: 40) make the following comments about discovery learning and direct teaching:

Discovery, related as it is to the satisfying of curiosity – a powerful drive in primary age children – can be highly motivating. . . . On the negative side, discovery can be enormously time-consuming, can sometimes lead to incorrect conclusions, and can follow numerous false trails.

Direct teaching, direct information-giving, has the advantage of allowing the teacher to cover a great deal of ground quickly, to control the subject matter being learned, to make sure it is correct and based on what has been learned by previous generations, and to short-cut a lot of anguish. The negative side is that children may merely be able to reproduce notions and facts that are ill-understood. The process may have engendered no commitment or excitement.

Kyriacou (1986) also writes of the dangers of lecturing on the grounds that young pupils cannot concentrate for very long. Exposition needs follow up involving action for pupils to make the material their own.

Sotto (1994: 123) quotes work by Rosenshine and Furst (1971) who described teaching behaviour which help children to learn as follows:

- being clear;
- being enthusiastic;
- using a variety of approaches;
- good questioning;
- being task-oriented (not wasting time);
- being indirect (not giving straight information);
- giving learners an opportunity to learn;
- making structuring comments (periodically summing up what has been done and signposting the way ahead).

Ofsted (1996: 30) stresses the importance of defining lesson objectives. 'The more clearly these expected outcomes are identified by the teacher, the more likely it is also that they will be appreciated by the pupils, so that both share a greater sense of purpose and awareness of making progress.' It also notes that 'Too often teachers do not vary their methods sufficiently. . . . The majority of good lessons consist of a blend of direct teaching to the whole class, to groups or individuals so that teaching closely matches their existing attainment and builds on it. . . . Where there is insufficient direct teaching, pupils may spend too much time on activities which contribute little to their knowledge, skills or understanding.'

However, Pollard (1994: 73) notes the 'need to avoid the sterile and simplistic divisions of approaches into whole-class versus individual teaching, single-subject versus topic-based, and recognise the importance of *fitness for purpose* and *flexibility* in approach'.

Reynolds *et al*. (1994: 17) write of systematic teaching which they describe as 'explicit, step by step instruction in which there is an emphasis upon all students practising correct responses and achieving academic success'.

Edwards and Mercer (1987) and Bennett and Kell (1989) all found that teachers were inclined not to give children information about what they were supposed to be learning, mainly because they did not want to limit the possibilities which might arise. They make the point that telling children what they are about to learn helps them to focus their attention and that it may be more effective to share goals with children.

Questioning

Questioning is a very important part of the process of teaching. It is not only a way of assessing whether children have learned the material under discussion but a way of stimulating thinking. There is a tendency for teachers to ask mainly questions which are tests of recall. The questions to be asked need to be prepared in broad outline before the lesson and it can be helpful to consider how many questions are open-ended and how many actually stimulate children to think more widely than simply to recall what has been learned. Galton *et al.* (1980) found that when the teachers in their study asked questions, 29.2 per cent were questions of fact, 18.3 per cent were closed questions and only 5 per cent were open questions, while 32.5 per cent referred to task supervision and 15 per cent to routine matters. Galton (1989) found that there were more higher-order questions used when the teacher was communicating with the whole class.

Perrott (1982: 47) defines higher- and lower-order questions as follows: 'Lower-order questions require the pupil to recall information. Higher-order questions require the pupil to manipulate information for some purpose.' She suggests that 'When your purpose is to require pupils to use information to either summarise, compare, contrast, explain, analyse, synthesise or evaluate use higher-order questions' (p. 254).

Sotto (1994) lists some of the kinds of questions which help children to think:

- questions which help learners to see links between facts and to identify patterns;
- questions which help learners to see why an inference may or may not be justified;
- questions which help learners to probe below the surface.

Waterhouse (1983: 84) advises that questions should build up to higher levels of thinking using 'how' and 'why' questions which he classifies as questions:

- using evidence to come to conclusions;
- applying rules and principles to specific instances;
- solving problems;
- using imagination;
- developing hypotheses to explain observations;
- evaluation.

However, Brophy and Good (1986: 363) state that 'The data do refute the simplistic (but frequently assumed) notion that higher-level questions are categorically better than lower-level questions. Several studies indicate that lower-level questions facilitate learning, even of higher-level objectives.' We can conclude that teachers need to use a variety of questions which stimulate thinking in a variety of ways. Askew and Williams (1995: 16) suggest that the effects of higher-order questions 'are more pronounced for understanding *concepts* and *principles* than for simple recall of facts'.

Kyriacou (1986) argues that teachers need to consider the type of thinking which questions are designed to promote. He notes that there are four key aspects of questioning:

- Quality – the clarity and appropriateness of the questions for their intended purpose.
- Targeting – the way teachers select pupils to answer questions, matching them to pupils.
- Interaction – techniques used by teachers to deliver questions and respond to pupils – eye contact, manner and tone of voice, use of pauses to give pupils thinking time, use of prompting, encouragement to elaborate answers.
- Feedback to pupils – the effect on pupils of questioning – answering questions is high risk because it is public and involves judgements about the answers; importance of encouragement.

Sometimes teachers want to assess how much a group knows about the subject under discussion and in this context may want to use rapid-fire questions. If the teacher wants to use questions to stimulate discussion then it is a good idea to pause before selecting a child to answer a question. The amount of time a teacher waits for an answer has an effect. Rowe (1974) found that if teachers wait for three or more seconds after asking a question various things happen:

- The length of the response increases.
- The number of the pupils' spontaneous answers and pertinent comments increases.
- The children's confidence when answering increases.
- The learners comment on each other's responses more frequently.
- Usually quiet learners respond more frequently.
- The learners ask more questions.

Perrott (1982: 57) suggests that it is a good idea to tell pupils why you are waiting after asking a question, using a verbal prompt such as 'Please think over your answer carefully.' She also suggests that if more thoughtful answers are required the teacher should praise those who give them.

Askew and Williams (1995: 17) note that increasing the wait time is only beneficial for higher-order questions. They also comment that 'when teachers make statements in order to provoke discussion rather than ask questions, pupils can display more complex thought, deeper personal involvement, wider participation, greater interconnectedness, and richer inquiry'.

Teachers need to be aware of the way they select children to answer questions. There is a tendency to select to answer children who sit within an inverted triangle with the teacher as its apex and to miss children who sit outside this area. There is also a natural tendency to ask those who are likely to have an answer and to omit those who are slower. This is partly because teachers do not want to embarrass slow-learning children and hold up the rest of the class because they are slow to answer, but inferences will be drawn from this and it is politic to include questions that such children will be able to answer and give them a chance to show this. Morgan and Saxton (1991) also found that some teachers tend to ask boys to answer more frequently than girls and vice versa.

All of this suggests that you need to check from time to time how you are distributing answers to questions. With older children you can get someone in the class to note for you the initials of those whom you ask to answer questions.

The way you actually respond to children's answers determines how ready they will be to risk answering in the future. You should make a point of praising answers which are good, especially where they show imagination or individual thinking. Dealing with wrong answers needs tact so that the self-esteem of the child concerned is preserved. Take the answer seriously when this is possible and praise anything which is positive in it. Give help in moving towards a correct answer using a series of prompts to guide the child towards the correct answer. Encourage children to respect the views of others. Morgan and Saxton (1991) suggest that sometimes a child gives a wrong answer because he or she has a different frame of reference from that of the teacher. In this context it is valuable to pursue the answer with questions like 'How do you know?' or 'Show me what you mean' in order to get at what the child is thinking.

Another aspect of the way you handle responses is the extent to which you use probing questions such as 'What makes you think that?', 'Can you tell us more about that?' The purpose of this is to make children think and to explore how much they actually know.

Perrot (1996) suggests that you need to give prior consideration to the way in which you will evaluate responses, particularly where higher-order questions are concerned.

Morgan and Saxton (1991: 80) suggest that 'The art of good questioning involves not only the ability to make and deliver good questions, it also involves active listening, thoughtful answers and, of equal importance, time to think. The key to good questioning is quality, not quantity.'

Discussion

Interactive teaching involves children in discussion with the teacher. This can be whole-class discussion or discussion with a group. Children can also discuss among themselves. The importance of discussion is that it is through verbalising learning that children make it their own. Mortimore *et al.* (1988: 269) make the point that 'there is no doubt that the quality of discourse in the classroom is one of the most important distinguishing features of effective teaching'. Questioning is often part of discussion with questions asked to stimulate thinking and to get the children interested in the topic to be dicussed. Ideally you should be trying to create a situation where children initiate talk.

Cooper and McIntyre (1996: 108) found that 'The fact that pupils were required to articulate their ideas in the discussion phase, also acted as stimulus for developing and fixing their ideas.' They go on to say, 'Pupils were virtually unanimous in describing the major value of groupwork as being, like class discussion, that it widened the pool of available ideas, and through this, enabled pupils to advance their thinking in ways which they could not achieve alone' (p. 109).

French (1987: 66) outlines the following characteristics of classroom talk:

- teachers do most of the talking;
- pupils are selected to speak rather than when they see fit;
- the teacher's part is mainly questioning pupils and evaluating answers;
- the pupils provide answers to questions rather than initiate talk.

If this is the case, the extent to which children are able to make learning their own through talk is limited and you need to consider whether there should be more opportunities for discussion. Tizard and Hughes (1984: 254) suggest that:

> The kind of dialogue that seems to help the child is not that currently favoured by many teachers in which the adult poses a series of questions. It is rather one in which the adult listens to the child's questions and comments, helps to clarify her ideas, and feeds her with the information she asks for.

Tizard and Hughes are writing about the learning needs of very young children. As children grow older their needs change but there is still an important place for listening to what they have to say. Richards (1987: 190) suggests that:

Children of all ages need to be given more opportunitites to pose questions, to offer explanations, to predict and speculate. They need greater encouragement to test their ideas through conducting experiments, designing structures, inventing artefacts or undertaking enquiries; through selecting and evaluating evidence and through establishing tentative conclusions, patterns and generalisations.

Kerry (1981: 63) notes that 'Teachers, consciously or unconsciously, signal to pupils how they want them to respond, and nowhere is this more significant than in discussion.' He goes on to say:

> To succeed at discussion the teacher needs to be genuinely interested in the topic, keen to involve pupils and accept their ideas, confident and relaxed. Unless these emotions and attitudes are real to the teacher, the teacher may give, and the pupils may read, the signals of boredom, insincerity, apprehension or tension in a way the individual might convey these in a normal conversation. Similarly a teacher may read these signals from the pupils if he or she is to respond genuinely to their mood.
>
> (Kerry 1981: 64)

Morgan and Saxton (1991: 114) advise having classroom rules for discussion sessions such as:

- take turns;
- listen attentively to others;
- keep to the point;
- give others a look in.

Topic work

Primary schools have over the years made a great deal of use of topics or projects which have tended to be cross-curricular. At its best this approach produced some outstanding work which was wide-ranging and involved children in initiating and carrying forward ideas of their own and presenting them in a variety of ways. Woods (1994: 169) suggests that very good projects created confidence and developed skills. 'Imagination and creativity have been stimulated but within a disciplined framework. They have learned skills of communicating in a variety of media.' At the other end of the scale there was probably a good deal of time wasted when teacher and children got bogged down in attempts to cover too much too superficially. Thomas (1993: 3) comments: 'If too much is attempted via general topics either important elements get neglected, or tenuous or even absurd links are made to secure their presence.' He goes on to say 'If a rigid subject division is manufactured, especially if each is taught by a different teacher, then overlap can be wastefully included, or, once again, items can be missed because they are assumed to be covered elsewhere.' Sammons *et al.* (1994: 54) note that 'there is evidence that topic-based approaches to the delivery of learning may lead to fragmentation in coverage of different subjects and can involve much routine low-level activity for pupils'.

Webb and Vulliamy (1996: 59) suggest a check-list for staff where topic work is concerned:

- Have staff agreed on the aims, intentions and purposes of topic teaching?
- What criteria are used to decide when and which subjects or aspects of subjects are taught through topics?
- Does the balance of subject elements in the topic over the year/key stage meet the National Curriculum requirements and the school's intentions?
- Are there lessons within a topic which address specific aspects of subjects?
- Are the key characteristics of each subject – concepts, skills, language – taught adequately?
- Is there an opportunity for pupils to contribute their own ideas to the direction or content of the topic?
- How is progression within particular subjects maintained from one topic to another?
- How is pupil progress in the subject elements monitored?
- How are topics evaluated?

Forward (1988) suggests that a plan should be made of the work to be covered in the project. It should include a statement of the aims of the project, giving the knowledge, skills and concepts to be covered and the aesthetic experiences and social and personal qualities it will foster. There should also be a chart giving the structure of the project which should be displayed in the classroom so that the children can see where they are going.

Projects are particularly valuable in giving purpose to small group work and to children working cooperatively. Children can be encouraged to plan work in their groups and decide what each member of the group will do. This needs clear directions about' how the group should work and is an opportunity for training group work skills. Groups can make a presentation to the class at the end of a project and this provides an opportunity to evaluate the work that has been done.

Projects give an opportunity for children to learn research skills and to learn to use books intelligently. It may involve using the Internet for information also. Bradley *et al.* (1985: 34) list the following skills which are developed through topic work:

- Accessing skills –   Know how to use a library and an index; to skim a page of print to locate information
- Comprehension skills – Skimming
       Looking for the main points
       Reading 'between the lines'
       Detecting bias in accounts
- Observation skills
- Recording skills –   Note taking
       Tabulation and drawing graphs
       Use of a tape recorder
       Use of a camera

Learning research skills tends to be more difficult than it seems and there is often a tendency for children to copy out passages from books rather than use them to find information which contributes to an overall view. Older children should be taught to put quotations in inverted commas so that they are aware of the extent to which they are quoting rather than summarising.

Printed material and information on computer should not be the only sources of information. It is important in topic work, as in most other work, for children to use first-hand sources of information, involving observing and asking questions. Field work is a valuable part of any topic and children should be encouraged to look closely, perhaps studying the buildings of their local environment, or looking at the flora and fauna of a chosen area. Studies of the local environment may include questioning older people about what they remember of the area in the past and this involves considering the questions which might be asked and how to word them so that good answers are obtained.

Projects are particularly valuable for developing language skills. Forward (1988: 84) lists the following uses of language which may be part of work on a project: 'recording, reporting, generalising, explaining, expressing opinions, regulating, justifying, presenting arguments, persuading, speculating, projecting, reflecting, expressing feelings, story telling, writing poetry'.

Projects should give rise to display which is gradually developed as the project proceeds. This can include booklets made by the children showing what they have learned as well as drawing and paintings, written work of various kinds, maps, charts and diagrams, models with explanations about how they came to be made and much else. Children should be involved in mounting the work and this provides an opportunity to help them to learn about what makes an attractive display.

Ofsted (1994a: 206) lists factors associated with successful topic work. These include the need to take account of National Curriculum requirements and the suggestions that 'Topics have a single subject or emphasise particular subjects.'

There is a need to consider progression in project work. Bradley *et al*. (1985: 23) suggest that progression could represent:

a)   increased complexity;
b)   increase in conceptual sophistication;
c)   an advance in the growth of interest.

Project work needs to be evaluated. There are many ways in which this can be done. If time could be found teachers could spend time evaluating each other's project work, using the displays and collections of children's work and spending time talking to the children about what they think they have learned. In one school teachers were expected to produce a report on each project, which was discussed with the headteacher. It is important to involve children in the evaluation process, perhaps in the way described earlier in this chapter. If there have been clear learning goals established at the beginning of work on a particular topic this makes the evaluation task easier for children and teacher.

The effect of the National Curriculum

The coming of the National Curriculum has affected the way teachers work in the classroom, particularly where project work is concerned, where history and geography are now more evident in many classrooms as subjects in their own right.

Muschamp *et al*. (1992) found that the teachers in their case study adapted and modified the National Curriculum to fit the way they wanted to work. The schools in their sample actively explored cross-curricular work in order to reduce pressures on the curriculum. They also felt that there was a good deal of pressure to move to a subject-based curriculum.

Sammons *et al*. (1994: 52) note that:

> There is some research evidence which indicates that teachers have great difficulty in successfully managing children's learning in sessions where work on several different curriculum areas is going on at the same time. In particular lower levels of work-related teacher-pupils communication and more routine and administrative interaction and lower levels of pupil engagement in work activity have been reported in primary school research studies. (Mortimore *et al*. 1988, Alexander 1992).

They also comment that 'Greater use of single ability grouping or streaming may be a potential consequence of the National Curriculum at Key Stage 2' (p. 54).

Woods (1995: 72) quotes a primary school teacher talking about using the National Curriculum 'as a baseline from which to grow, not to become slaves to it, but to actually use it and adapt it in the ways that suit our philosophy and don't perhaps narrow our outlook too much'.

Cox and Sanders (1994: 63) found teachers of the youngest children expressing concern that 'such pressure had led to a reduction in their opportunities for free play and less time for their teachers to talk with them and thereby help to enrich their language'. On the other hand, the headteachers they talked to noted benefits such as a broader curriculum with more science than previously. There was also the danger that very young children might be introduced too early to formal teaching.

They found that the National Curriculum gave positive benefits to the more able, 'in particular the richer variety of subject matter to which the children were exposed, including more science and the greater opportunities for pupils to carry out investigations for themselves' (p. 68). At the same time they found concern about slow learners. 'The quality of these children's grasp of the basic skills and concepts was seen to be threatened by the weight of the wider curriculum demands and the drive towards average levels of performance in the various attainment targets' (p. 75).

Galton (1998) surveyed work in thirty-eight primary schools using the same tests as he and colleagues had used in the Oracle study of sixty schools in 1976–8 comparing children's performance in Years 4, 5 and 6. He found that the scores on mathematics, language and reading had declined significantly, with the greatest decline in reading. Mathematical concepts were better in Year 6 and there was an improvement in use of capitals and punctuation in all three year groups. He found that there had been an increase in whole-class teaching and the use of group work and there was less individual work. However, overall standards had fallen and he suggests that some of this decline must be due to the introduction of the National Curriculum. He suggests that this had reduced the time teachers spent hearing children read and the amount of immediate feedback children were given while writing. There had also been increased emphasis on subject specialism and a decline in topic work involving more than one subject area.

Osborn (1996: 35) records that an experienced infant teacher found 'in comparison with the past her planning and organisation had become very focused on covering specific areas of knowledge, and making sure that all attainment targets were covered'. A second teacher 'felt that the needs of the slower children in her class were not being met by the National Curriculum, and that there had been a loss of spontaneity and fun in her teaching'.

Homework

Primary schools are increasingly setting homework of some kind for children. For the youngest children this may be an arrangement with parents to hear children read for a short time each day. For older children homework may have various purposes. The DfEE paper on homework (1998b: 8) gives the following purposes:

- developing an effective partnership between the school and parents and other carers in pursuing the aims of the school;
- consolidating and reinforcing skills and understanding, particularly in literacy and numeracy;
- exploiting resources for learning, of all kinds, at home;
- extending school learning, for example through additional reading;
- encouraging pupils as they get older to develop the confidence and self discipline needed to study on their own, and preparing them for the requirements of secondary school.

This paper suggests that there should be a regular programme so that children and their parents know what to expect each week. Children need to be very clear about what they are to do and they need feedback on their work. This need not necessarily be straightforward marking. Homework might be learning spellings or tables for a test or preparing a presentation to a group or to the whole class.

7

CLASSROOM MANAGEMENT

Teaching approaches

Over the past few years there has been considerable pressure on teachers to do less individual work and more work in a whole-class situation, and less topic work in which subjects are integrated. Teachers have also been coping with the introduction of the National Curriculum and seeking out ways of working within its confines which are in accord with their values and beliefs about primary school learning and teaching.

Alexander *et al.* (1992: 28) note that 'research studies show relatively low gains in pupil understanding in classrooms where teachers structure the day largely in terms of individual teaching'. They also note that 'whole-class teaching is associated with higher-order questioning, explanations and statements, and these in turn correlate with higher levels of pupil peformance'. On the other hand, they also report that:

> Observational studies show that pupils pay attention and remain on task when being taught as a class but may, in fact, slow down their rate of working to meet the teacher's norm, thus narrowing the challenge of what is taught to an extent which advocates of whole-class teaching might well find uncomfortable.

They suggest (p. 29) that on many occasions 'grouping pupils within the class enables resources to be shared, fosters the social development which primary schools rightly believe to be an essential part of their task and, above all, provides for pupils to interact with each other and with their teacher'.

Forward (1988: 19, 20), writing of work in small primary schools where a class may contain more than one age group, suggests that even in this situation there are occasions for whole-class teaching such as the following:

- Oral and written work when the emphasis is on the expression of opinion, justification, description and narrative and the response can be at a level appropriate to the individual pupil.
- Language or mathematics when certain basic concepts and skills which need regular reinforcement and repetition throughout the primary phase are being taught.

- Initiating and motivating thematic project work as well as ongoing explanation, summarising and concluding this work.
- Reading stories, enjoying verse, singing and making music, physical education, some types of two and three dimensional art and certain other practical activities.

One might add to these situations where instructions about safety are concerned.

Galton (1989: 7) points out that research findings on direct teaching 'where the teacher instructed pupils about what to do as opposed to indirect methods where they responded to pupils' initiatives have been going on for a long time but no results produced superiority for direct methods'. In a later publication (Galton and Patrick 1990: 178) he notes that:

> Research in the United States has . . . shown that the direct instruction approach, while very suitable for teaching basic subjects such as reading, writing and computation, is far less successful for the kinds of tasks which best develop these 'higher-order' thinking skills. According to some recent research by Jennifer Nias (1988) these tasks require teachers to foster a kind of relationship with their pupils which is very different from the form of dependency which the direct instruction model deliberately sets out to create.

The conclusion that can be drawn from all these writers is that you need to use a mixture of approaches, using direct teaching when it is appropriate, remembering that this is one of the opportunities the teacher has to have contact with all the children. On other occasions it may be better to work with groups of children or individuals depending on the work you are doing.

There is some evidence that too much individual work spreads the teacher as a resource too thinly and in any case tends not to be the kind of stimulus envisaged in the Plowden Report (Central Advisory Council for Education 1967). Gipps (1992: 19) suggests that:

> All the evidence points to the fact that when teachers take as their main focus individual children most of their interactions are routine, organisational and low-level; the children, by contrast, get little teacher attention, working mostly on their own. As a result extended discussions with children about the tasks – including higher-order questions and statements – are severely limited.

You will also have to decide on the extent to which you teach single subjects and the extent to which you integrate the curriculum. Some teachers also plan work so that groups of children or individuals are working on different subjects at the same time. Pollard (1994: 52) suggests that it is likely that the National Curriculum will lead to increased single subject teaching.

Mortimore *et al.* (1988: 229) also found that 'when the pupil's day was given a structure or framework such that children were given single tasks to undertake over fairly short periods of time such as a lesson or an afternoon, and were encouraged to manage the completion of the tasks independently of the teacher, the impact was positive for a range of cognitive and non-cognitive outcomes'.

Grouping for learning

Differentiation

One of the most difficult tasks for the teacher is to provide for the wide range of ability which is present even in the most homogeneous class. Webb and Vulliamy (1996: 45) suggest that primary teachers can use three possible approaches to differentiation:

- The provision for the able of additional more demanding work in the same area once they had completed that set for the class.
- The allocation of completely different activities for pupils of different abilities.
- Setting the same task for all pupils but expecting a range of outcomes in terms of speed of task completion, quality and quantity of work and the amount of help required.

Mortimore *et al.* (1988: 230) found that 'where pupils worked on the same task as other pupils of roughly the same ability, or when all the pupils worked within the same curriculum area but on different tasks at their own level, the effect upon progress was positive'. If everyone was working on exactly the same task the effect was negative. This must depend on the type of task given. If it is open-ended as envisaged by Webb and Vulliamy, who suggest that the end product might be differentiated by requiring different forms of presentation, the effect could be positive.

Another way of coping with differences is to group children by ability for some work. With older children this may be done by setting across the year group but it may also be a matter of grouping within the class. The National Numeracy Project (1997) suggests that for mathematics there should be possibly four groups and no more than five. Some teachers will be concerned that such grouping does not affect the self-esteem of those in the lowest ability group.

Askew and Williams (1995: 40) writing of grouping for mathematics found the following:

- attainment grouping improves pupils' attitudes towards the subject but does not affect attitude towards school;
- any effects on self-esteem are small: positive for low-attainers and slightly negative for others.

They also found that for low attainers 'seeing someone of similar attainment cope is more motivating than seeing mastery'.

Scheerens (1992: 41) quotes a wide-ranging American study which found that 'Studies on streaming or working with ability groups indicate that this type of teaching works more positively with more gifted pupils, and that with less able groups, taking the average results of large numbers of surveys, hardly any effect was found.'

Reynolds et al. (1994: 28) quote from a Norwegian study of setting which found that 'students with low socioeconomic status and students from rural areas were the losers'. The HMI survey of combined and middle schools (DES 1985b) found that 'no association was identified between setting in English and mathematics and the quality of pupils' work in these subjects' (p. 65, para. 7.3). Ofsted (1994b) found that teachers who achieved high standards used ability grouping effectively.

Overall there would seem to be mixed views from research about the effects of ability grouping but in practical terms there is much to be said for it. It is very difficult to provide for the needs of thirty or more children on an individual basis and grouping by ability makes provision a little easier. However, it is important that you bear in mind the possibility that the less able children may lose in terms of self-esteem. It may be worth, from time to time, discussing with them their feelings about being in groups.

Other forms of grouping

Children need the opportunity to mix with others of varying ability and this means that some work needs to be in mixed ability groups. Bennett and Dunne (1992: 118) found that mixed ability groups were more satisfactory for collaborative work. Low ability groups are a drain on the teachers' time and less able children do not have the stimulus which more able peers provide. They found that low-attainers 'who were involved in mixed ability groups, gave evidence of being enabled to work more successfully through cooperation with more able peers'. They also suggest that friendship grouping is not necessarily the best solution since children need to mix with a variety of other people. Friendship groups, particularly at Key Stage 2 are likely to be single sex and tend to be children of similar ability although this is not always the case. There is some evidence that with infants mixed gender groups are more effective than single sex groups but as children grow older they tend to develop negative views about this. Ideally children should experience being in a variety of groups for different aspects of their work.

Organising the classroom

One of your main tasks as the teacher is to organise the work of the class-room so that the learning is as effective as possible. The decisions you make about how you organise will depend to a large extent on your beliefs about:

- how far you want the work to be child-centred;
- your teaching intentions and any constraints which affect you;
- your personal style of teaching and the learning styles of your children;
- how you see the children's ability and your view of their previous experience;
- the relationships you want to develop with your children.

Alexander *et al.* (1992: 31) suggest that:

> It is important for teachers to organise their classrooms so that they have the opportunity to interact with their pupils: to offer explanations which develop thinking, to encourage speculation and hypothesis through sensitive questioning, to create, above all, a climate of interest and purpose.

They also suggest that the teacher needs to understand how individual pupils are thinking and thus be in a position to influence that thinking. You need to consider how the way you organise affects this kind of relationship with children and the amount and quality of interaction you achieve with the children.

Boydell (1978: 75) describes a study in which the interactions of six teachers were observed in detail. The study found that:

> High-level cognitive contributions involving ideas, explanations and problems accounted for about one tenth of the teacher's total conversation. Moreover, open-ended questions about the children's work activities (where the teacher was prepared to accept a wide range of ideas and solutions) were rarely encountered.

She goes on to summarise the problems which arise when there is too much emphasis on individual attention:

- some children get very little – chances are unequal;
- the intellectual level of contacts is low;
- children get too little contact with a range of language.

Use of time

A very important part of organisation is the use of time. You cannot increase the time available, only look for better ways of using it. All teachers occasionally need to look at the way they use time to see if they are making the best use of this resource.

There have been many studies of teachers' use of time. Galton (1989: 45) found the following:

> Primary teachers were engaged in some form of interaction with pupils for over 78 per cent of the time during which they were under observation. During this period, over 70 per cent of these interactions were with individual pupils and just under 20 per cent were with the whole class, leaving around 9½ per cent of observed occasions when the teacher talked to a group of pupils. The 20 per cent accounted for ¾ of the attention that an individual pupil received from the teacher.

Tizard *et al.* (1988) found that in the top infant classes less than half the day was devoted to work activity. Forty-three per cent of the day was spent on routine activities such as registration, visits to the toilet, lining up, tidying up and on meals and playtimes. Children were on-task for 66 per cent of their time.

Hargreaves (1990: 78), in a later study, found better on-task behaviour in small primary schools:

> The striking feature of both the infant and junior records is the high level of task work. Seventy-one per cent of observations were task-focused, and this increased to 80 per cent if routine task-supporting jobs, such as sharpening pencils or ruling lines were included. Only 13 per cent of the observations were coded as off-task or distracted behaviour such as chatting or day-dreaming. In the Oracle study [Galton *et al.* 1980] the equivalent proportions were 64 per cent task work, 17 per cent routine jobs and 19 per cent distraction.

Hargreaves notes that the children in small primary schools apparently 'worked harder and talked less than their Oracle counterparts, but when they did so, the topic was more often about their work' (p. 82).

Alexander (1992: 69), working as evaluator of a project in Leeds which set out to improve performance in primary schools, found that on average children in the classrooms where observation took place spent:

- 59 per cent of their time working;
- 11 per cent on associated routine activities (getting out and putting away books and apparatus, sharpening pencils and so on);

- 8 per cent waiting for attention from the teacher or other adult;
- 21 per cent distracted from the task which had been set;
- 1 per cent other (unspecified).

He goes on to suggest that 'Teachers need to look at both the frequency and the proportion of their interactions in considering how to make the best use of the strictly limited time for interacting with their pupils' (p. 77).

Mortimore *et al.* (1988: 228) found that:

> The amount of teacher time spent interacting with the class (rather than with individuals or groups) had a significant positive relationship with progress in a wide range of areas. In contrast, where a high proportion of the teacher's time was spent communicating with individual pupils, a negative impact was recorded.

If you are to manage time well you need to give consideration to how you are actually using it. It is helpful to plan the way time will be used in any lesson and then to consider how you actually used it. Classrooms are busy places and it is not really possible to chart the way you are using time with any accuracy but it is helpful to think back over a morning or afternoon and look critically at how you have used the time available. How much time did you spend working with the whole class, with groups and with individuals? How far did what actually happened conform to your original plan for the use of time? Did you do anything which children could have done for themselves if you had introduced it differently? How much time was spent on routine tasks and how much time did the children actually spend on task? Could you increase this by preparing better?

In addition to looking at how you are spending your own time, you need to be concerned with how the children are spending their time. One way in which time is often wasted is in queueing to see the teacher. Wheldall and Glynn (1989: 51) made a study of queueing in a primary classroom. They found that 'On average about three children were observed to be waiting at any one time, varying from zero to twenty-one children waiting in classes of approximately thirty children.' They also found that 'The mean length of time spent waiting was about one and a half minutes, but this was highly variable, ranging from zero (when children received immediate attention) to over thirteen minutes. . . . A quarter of the teachers were observed to have at least one child in their class waiting for more than ten minutes.'

It is easy to see that time spent in this way soon adds up and you need to consider ways in which you can reduce the need to queue. Are you doing enough to make children independent learners? Have you enough material around the room which children can use to refer to or check whether they are doing the right thing? Could you more often suggest that children who are waiting to see you should work at something else until you are free?

Another possibility is to encourage children to do more to help each other, suggesting to them that they should approach another child in their group before coming to you. Another aspect of planning time from the teacher's point of view is to see that when you wish to work with one group of children others have work which does not demand a great deal of attention from you.

In trying to help children to use their time well, particularly with older children, it is useful to train them to plan their work and estimate how long something is going to take. The ability to plan work over time and work independently is something which needs training. It is useful to discuss with children how they can best organise their work over a short period. Most children will have tasks they prefer to some other tasks and they need to be encouraged to do the tasks they like least first, saving the ones they like to do later, on the grounds that they will probably do the ones they like doing more quickly. They also need to do the tasks they dislike doing while they are fresh. It is also a good idea to suggest to the children that they estimate how long each task is going to take and check how they are doing as time goes on. Work on training these skills can start with giving children the choice of the order in which they do two tasks and perhaps increase this to three or more over time.

Seating patterns

Children in primary school classes have for a long time been seated in groups. Galton et al. (1980) found that very little use was made of this form of seating for working cooperatively. Ninety per cent of the teachers in their study never used group work for single subject teaching and 69 per cent did not use it for art and craft or topic work. Only 10 per cent of teachers observed actually used cooperative group work. Some children never experienced it at all.

Wheldall and Glynn (1989: 59) studied two Year 3 classes of twenty-eight and twenty-five children. The classes were observed for two weeks in seating round tables looking at the amount of on-task behaviour which took place. 'This was defined, by the teacher, as doing what the teacher had instructed. . . . The observation schedules provided estimates of on-task behaviour for each child for each lesson, which, when averaged, gave an estimate of on-task behaviour for the whole class.'

Desks were then moved into rows without comment from the teacher and children were observed for a further two weeks. Finally desks were moved back to their original position for two weeks. They found that:

> The on-task behaviour of the first class rose from an average of 72 per cent to 85 per cent in rows and fell back to 73 per cent when tables seating was resumed. Similarly, the second class rose from averaging 68 per cent on-task behaviour during baseline (tables) to 92 per cent during rows, and fell to 73 per cent for the final tables phase.

The most marked effect was on children whose on-task behaviour was initially low. For these children increases of 30 per cent were not uncommon. The children themselves said they preferred seating in rows.

Bennett and Blundell (1983) had similar findings. They found that both the children's involvement in their work and the quantity of work completed rose significantly when the children were moved in rows rather than groups.

This evidence suggests that teachers would be well advised to work in rows rather than groups. However, if cooperative work is to be done in groups the seating in rows is less convenient although it is not difficult to form groups of four by turning chairs round. It is also difficult to carry on class discussions when children cannot see each other. An alternative which may have some of the advantages of seating in rows is to seat children in a horseshoe. This allows every child to see others in class discussion and is not difficult to rearrange for group work.

Wheldall and Glynn also studied the effect of mixed sex seating. In a Year 4 class studied the level of on-task behaviour was 90 per cent during mixed sex seating and fell to 76 per cent when same sex seating was introduced. It rose again to 89 per cent when mixed sex seating was resumed. There was also a lower rate of disruption. However, they point out that 'What the results of this study does not show is whether the rises in on-task levels were accompanied by increases in the quantity and quality of academic work produced' (p. 64). They also found that 'Subsequent discussion with the pupils revealed that in general they felt they concentrated less when seated next to (same sex) friends, and that they had worked harder during the intervention phase' (p. 65).

Mixed sex seating would undoubtedly be unpopular with children at the junior school stage but it might be worth experimenting to see whether the same results are repeated. The samples in all these studies are very small.

Working with other adults

There is an increasing tendency for schools to employ teaching assistants and also to involve parents in helping in the classroom, particularly with the younger children. It is important to see that any other adults involved are properly briefed by the teacher so that they are fulfilling the teacher's aims. Moyles (1992: 148) makes the following comments about the use of helpers in the classroom: 'Helpers should, like the children, be clear about what they are doing, why they are doing it and what benefits it has to the children and the teacher. The children need to be told what the adult's role is and how the children are expected to interact and behave.' She suggests that helpers should be given written information explaining the objectives of the tasks they are being asked to undertake and what they should look for. The school also needs guidelines for helpers, written in a sensitive and sympathetic style.

Helpers need unobtrusive training. This may be done in discussing work with them before and after the lesson, by drawing things to their attention as work proceeds and after it is finished. An important point to stress at the beginning of their work and to write into school instructions for helpers is the necessity for confidentiality. They will see and hear things and observe the children of parents they may know and must not discuss these things outside the school.

There are other ways in which adults other than the teacher can contribute to the children's learning. There may be parents of other nationalities who could talk to the children about their home countries or in schools where there are children with languages other than English, parents may come in to tell stories in their home language to younger children. There is also a valuable place for writers of children's books and artists and craftsmen and women coming to talk about their work.

The classroom environment

Rollisson (1990: 1) suggests that:

> Children need opportunities to apply skills if they are to learn thoroughly. In order to apply skills effectively, children need an environment in which learning is irresistible; one which provides the necessary motivation; one in which the process of learning is so exciting that they recognise the need to acquire certain skills in order to participate fully in what is on offer.

This is something of a council of perfection which can be seen as something to aim for. She goes on to suggest that if this is to be achieved organisation in the classroom needs:

- well organised and structured resources;
- a system which children know how to operate;
- a range of supplementary activities;
- effective use of classroom space;
- an established routine that tasks begun are completed, though not necessarily to a time limit.

(Rollisson 1990: 7)

The classroom environment is an important tool for the teacher. A well-organised and attractive environment tempts children into learning and provides stimulus for discussion. It can be useful to ask oneself whether if the children were left to their own devices for a time, they would be able to continue to spend that time profitably because of the provision in the classroom environment.

The organised environment helps both the teacher and the children to use time well by the way materials for work are structured so that children can move from one piece of work to the next without always needing to consult the teacher and by displaying information which children need for their work. It also provides a way of recognising individual children's work through display. Display can also provide an opportunity for children, particularly older children to learn the art of displaying work.

Alexander (1992: 31) describes the way in which the Leeds study involved teachers teaching together. He notes that this has 'potential to provide a major corrective to the inconsistencies in curriculum expertise and delivery which are such a widespread and unsatisfactory feature of the primary school class teacher system'. He sees teachers teaching together as a powerful device for promoting curriculum development.

Teachers may work together as a permanent team or come together for parts of the curriculum. A pair of classes may share a visit and work together to develop the outcome of the experience. A year group may plan work together and each teacher then carry out the plans with his or her own class. There are many possibilities and all of them make a wider range of expertise available to the children. Working together is particularly valuable for inexperienced teachers who have the opportunity to learn from more experienced colleagues.

Control in the classroom

The Elton Report, Discipline in Schools (DES 1989a: 88), made the following comment:

> When we visited schools we were struck by the difference in their 'feel' or atmosphere. Our conversations with teachers left us convinced that some schools have a more positive atmosphere than others. It was in these positive schools that we tended to see the work and behaviour which impressed us most. We found that we could not explain these different school atmospheres by saying that the pupils came from different home backgrounds. Almost all the schools we visited were in what many teachers would describe as difficult urban areas. We had to conclude that these differences had something to do with what went on in the schools themselves.

If teaching and learning is to be effective the teacher must be in control of what happens in the classroom. The ability to do this in ways which still leave children able to take initiatives and work independently takes time to acquire and you have to discover your personal style. It helps to observe other teachers at work and class control is something else which can be learned from example when teachers work together.

Kyriacou (1991: 85) suggests that your authority as a teacher depends largely on four main aspects of your role:

- conveying your status;
- teaching competently;
- exercising managerial control;
- dealing with pupil misbehaviour effectively.

He goes on to say:

> Behaving as though you have status will be conveyed in your appearing relaxed, self-assured and confident, as indicated by your tone of voice, posture, facial expression and use of eye contact. When you issue an instruction, your tone will indicate by its matter-of-factness that you simply expect without question that the instruction will be followed.
>
> (Kyriacou 1991: 85)

He also suggests that 'If you convey to pupils that you are knowledgeable about the topic or subject, are interested in it, and can set up the learning actvities skilfully, then pupils will respect your ability to teach: this will confirm your authority to manage their behaviour' (p. 87).

There are a number of principles about classroom control which are worth remembering:

- *Children behave badly when they don't know what to do.* It is important to organise work so that everyone is clear what he or she should be doing, particularly when you are changing activities.
- *Always get attention before giving instructions.* It is a good idea with any class to agree at an early stage, a signal that you want attention and then to insist that children react to it. It could be something as simple as clapping your hands. Be careful to give instructions clearly and to reinforce important points.
- *Be ready when children come into the classroom.* It is a good idea to establish a pattern that children come in and immediately start work on something straightforward. This could be from instructions written on the board or ongoing work.
- *Be individual in calling children to order.* When you are trying to get attention it is better to name individuals than to make comments to the class generally. It is generally more effective to single out those who are doing the right things for praise rather than commenting on those not attending, though this may be necessary also. It is a good idea to check how you do this from time to time to see whether you are being more negative than positive.

- *Learn to scan the class.* Good teachers continually look round the class. Beginners often get absorbed with an individual or a group and forget to check on what is happening elsewhere.

Kounin (1970) studied the way teachers managed their classes. He noted the way that when a teacher reprimanded an individual child, this had an effect on the other children. He found that punishment and firmness increased attention only in classes where the children had high motivation to learn. It had no impact where the motivation was low.

He identified various aspects of teacher behaviour which were effective in managing children. The first of these he called 'withitness' which he describes as 'the teacher's communicating to the children by her actual behaviour that she knows what the children are doing, or has the proverbial eyes at the back of her head' (p. 81). Effective teachers were also able to deal with more than one issue at once. They moved smoothly from one activity to another without slowing down or going back and forth between activities. They were not easily deflected from the main activity.

In Chapter 5 we saw that teachers needed to set up rules for classroom behaviour at an early stage with a new class, discuss these with the children and insist on conformity. Children need to see the purpose of these rules so that they can see the reason for them.

Control in the classroom is most difficult at points of change of activity and as pupils come in and pack away at the end of lessons. You can anticipate these problems by making sure that you prepare for changes of activity and give careful and well thought-out instructions.

Body language

Control in the classroom depends a good deal on body language, both your behaviour and your reading of the way children react. It helps if you are aware of your non-verbal communication and of the signals which the children give you. Many of these are used in everyday life without people being aware that they are reading non-verbal signals. Neill and Caswell (1993: 9) suggest that 'Non-verbal communication includes face-to-face interaction, actual behaviour and signals, such as dress and room arrangement which you or the children may "set up" before you meet each other, also facial expression, gaze, head and body posture, hand movements, interpersonal distance and spacing, intonation and pace of speech.'

You communicate a good deal by the way you use language. Kyriacou (1986: 6) makes the following point about the teacher's language:

The teacher's language conveys – through the types of phrases used, its tone, and how and when it is used – a whole range of messages to pupils about the teacher's perceptions and expectations regarding learning and teaching. What is now apparent is that pupils pick up such messages with great sophistication and often with consequences which the teacher may not intend.

Cohen and Manion (1983: 231) make a similar point. 'If children detect discrepancies between what a teacher says and what he actually does, they will ignore what he says and be affected much more by what he does. Further if they see discrepancies between what he says, he expects and what he allows, they will tend to be influenced by what he allows.'

The teacher's tone of voice is important in establishing control in the classroom. You need to sound relaxed and natural if you want to create a relaxed atmosphere. A quiet voice is more effective than a loud one and any teacher who has experienced losing his or her voice and going on teaching will know that the children will often react to this by speaking very quietly also.

Neill and Caswell (1993: 79) say that 'Fumbling and self-grooming are among a whole range of nervous tics which teachers are often blissfully unaware of while their classes are only too aware.'

Children react well when you make eye contact with them and react attentively to eye contact when they tell you something. Smiling helps to create a relaxed atmosphere and also shows that you like them.

Human beings tend to keep a certain distance from each other and different cultures have different customs about this. Moving closer to someone intensifies the message you want to give so that if you move closer to a child to offer praise this is likely to be more appreciated. Similarly if you move closer to reprimand a child this is likely to be seen as more threatening and so more effective. A forward leaning posture tends to communicate greater involvement and a more friendly approach.

Neill and Caswell (1993: 129) write of dominance and threat:

> *Dominance* is the ability to control or influence the behaviour of others. *Threat* is behaviour which indicates that there is a risk of physical attack (i.e. an escalated confrontation) unless the opponent gives way. Dominance does *not* imply confrontation; in fact if dominance is well established the subordinate will give way without any confrontation. Threat indicates that dominance is not fully established, and the more extreme the threat, the greater the risk to dominance.

As teacher you demonstrate dominance when you stand above a child who is sitting. To create a more equal situation you may crouch down beside a child. A raised chin also indicates dominance. Standing with hands on hips tends to be threatening though Neill and Caswell found that children perceived it as 'irritable' or 'impatient'. They also found that 'folding the arms gives the same impression as refusing to budge, but is less threatening because the arms now form a barrier in front of the body' (p. 83). Pacing to and fro is distracting. You can use these postures to meet particular situations.

They also studied hand gestures and suggest that 'Lack of gestures indicate lack of involvement with and mastery of the ideas being communicated and thus gives a clear signal to the class that you are not on top of your subject' (p. 117).

You also need to be aware of the children's body language particularly any which suggests that misbehaviour is about to start. Children who are likely to disrupt the lesson tend to keep a wary eye on the teacher and may look round the class to locate potential allies. They may sit with their heads low trying to conceal their activity from you. You may prevent any disruption by moving towards the children in question and making it clear that you are aware of what they are doing.

Behaviour modification

This is an important way of managing a class. Wheldall and Glynn (1989: 17, 18) make the following points about it:

1   Teaching is concerned with the observable.
    Teachers who adopt a behavioural approach concern themselves with what children actually do, i.e. their behaviour, rather than speculating about unconscious motives or the processes underlying their behaviour.
2   Almost all classroom behaviour is learned.
    The sorts of child behaviour that teachers are likely to be concerned with are almost all learned as a result of interactions with home, classroom and school environment.
3   Learning involves change in behaviour.
    The only way we know (that we can know) that learning has taken place is by observing changes in behaviour.
4   Behaviour changes as a result of consequences.
5   Altering the context can change behaviour.

The techniques of behaviour modification can be used to deal with the behaviour of a particular child or a group or the whole class. The case of a child who was continually disrupting other children's work was described in Chapter 4 (pp. 34–5).

A similar approach can be used to change the behaviour of the whole class. The starting point is to observe the behaviour you want to change very carefully, looking at what led up to it, how often it occurs, when it occurs and in what situations. Suppose your class tend to come into the room very noisily and take time to settle down after the morning break and you want to train them to come in quietly and start work immediately. Most teachers deal with this by reproving the noisy children and telling them to settle down. Try instead to praise those who are coming in quietly and starting work. Explain to the class that you want to improve the way they come in and that you are going to look particularly for those who come in quietly. At the same time observe which children are the noisy ones and keep a list of them over a few days. Make a point of praising any improvement in the behaviour of the children on your list and talk individually to any who appear not to be making any effort. Look for a way you can reward the whole class if they succeed in coming in quietly for several days. This might be an opportunity to do something they particularly enjoy.

Dealing with children who pose problems

Most teachers from time to time will encounter children who pose particular problems of behaviour. This is especially so since many children who would formerly have been in special schools are now in mainstream classes. Winkley (1990: 77) suggests that the school should have three principle objectives:

i)   that the school and the parent, working together in the child's best interest, create an environment in which the child feels secure and valued;

ii) that children gain insight into their own difficulties and learn how to decide for themselves how best to fulfil their talents and aspirations;

iii) that the contentment and stability which arises from the first point leads to fulfilment and positive achievement in the pupil's academic and social life.

He goes on to suggest that the school needs to keep careful records of progress. 'It means monitoring the pupil by clearly observing his behaviour and showing sensitive and insightful understanding of development.' He suggests that it may be useful to write a short review of the pupil's progress each week which might be shown to the child and his or her parents. It should emphasise positive achievement, however small, whether this is in work, social behaviour or atttitude. 'A sense of . . . caring is created through the accumulation of small signs: friendly contacts, commending, noticing, asking opinions, always speaking politely and thoughtfully, smiling. These build into a powerful set of clues and impressions' (p. 83).

Docking (1992) lists a number of ways in which teachers see the troublesome pupil. They may attribute the child's behaviour to his or her bad motives and intentions. This allows them to exempt themselves from any blame and convey the message to the child that he or she needs to take the first step.

Another approach is to blame the home for the child's behaviour. This again exempts you from looking to see whether your own behaviour is contributing to the situation. Behaviour in school is certainly affected by school factors as well as home factors and these need examining.

The pupil may also be seen 'as functioning within a network of inter-related systems such as the family, the peer group, the classroom, the playground and the school at large. Each system is made up of interacting elements, or aspects of the situation, which influence, and are often influenced by, the child's behaviour' (p. 17).

Dealing with confrontation

One of the most difficult things to deal with is outright confrontation. A child refuses to do what you ask or perhaps swears at you and you have the rest of the class watching keenly to see what you will do.

When this sort of thing occurs you usually need to think on your feet. It is important not to react aggressively or in a threatening manner however furious you may feel. You need to act in a calm way and look for an escape route for you both. One way of reacting is to try to separate the child from the audience. It may be possible to take him or her out of the room, saying something like, 'Let's go and talk this over.' When you get outside you can ask what the problem was about and why the child became so angry. Try to sound sympathetic rather than indignant. This approach has the advantage of ending the drama. When you bring the child back into the classroom you should deal with him or her in a matter of fact way perhaps talking about work in a positive manner.

Another approach is to assert your authority. You can demonstrate blank astonishment that anyone should behave in such a way. You can also produce a show of anger, moving towards the child and keeping eye contact. In this situation it is easier to stay in control if you are acting rather than really feeling angry. This is a somewhat risky approach since the child may react defiantly and you are still left with the situation.

If the behaviour is not very serious you may choose to pass it off lightly, perhaps saying something like 'I'm sure you didn't really mean that. Would you like to think again?'

Sometimes the child in question is one who is recognised by everyone as tending to behave abnormally. In this case you may choose to ignore the behaviour and concentrate instead upon the child's work, acting as if he or she has asked for help or finding something good to say about it.

All confrontation issues are better dealt with away from an audience. It may be a good idea to talk to the child at break time or lunch time. Try to find out why he or she reacted in that particular way. Show a caring and concerned attitude and talk about how it made you feel, trying to get the child to see things from another point of view.

91

8

WORKING IN GROUPS

In the last chapter we looked at ability grouping as a way of managing the diversity of ability and needs within the class. There is also an important place for collaborative work in groups. The process of assimilating some new learning is helped considerably by talking about it and comparing one's own understanding with that of others. Children also learn in many ways from each other and the good teacher needs to harness children's readiness to talk to each other to their learning.

Webb and Vulliamy (1996: 37) quote Reid *et al.* (1987) who list some of the advantages of getting children to work together in groups. They can:

- generate more ideas in a collaborative setting;
- explain, question and learn from each other using the language and patterns of interaction;
- recognise the value of their own experience in acquiring and developing new knowledge;
- develop confidence in themselves as learners and in sharing ideas with a critical audience;
- develop an awareness of the differences between exploratory talk and an oral presentation;
- generate feelings of responsibility to the group and encourage self-discipline.

Bennett and Dunne (1992: 23) note that learning to work in groups has advantages for future employment 'First, as a means of forging and sustaining interpersonal relations (e.g. building morale, team spirit, solving interpersonal problems, managing work groups etc.) and second, as an effective means of solving work-related problems (e.g. generating ideas, increasing productivity, pooling areas of expertise, and communicating ideas).'

Bennett and Dunne also note that group work can help to free teachers from constant low level demands if the children are encouraged to use their group as a reference point and approach the teacher for information only if the group cannot help. Teachers found that demands on them fell dramatically when children were 'not allowed to make requests to the teacher until all the possibilities of finding an answer had been exhausted in the group' (p. 52).

Harwood (1988: 242) lists some of the effects of collaborative learning on personal and social development:

- Cooperative learning techniques have strong and consistent effects on relationships between children of different ethnic backgrounds.
- Mutual concern among pupils is increased regardless of the structure used.
- There is some evidence that self-confidence and self-esteem are improved.
- Pupils in classes using cooperative learning generally report increased liking of school.

He goes on to quote work by Tann (1981) who looked at ninety-six examples of group work and found a lack of questioning and risk-taking. Tann also found that there were a number of silent members and some fooling around by low-ability older boys. Harwood concludes that while there are obviously gains in group work there can be dangers. Teachers need to be cautious and observe what is happening very carefully.

Although teachers have often seen the advantages of collaborative group work many have been slow to make use of it. The Oracle study (Galton *et al.* 1980: 70) found that 'though the children are typically seated in groups, for the great majority of time they work as *individuals* concentrating on their own, individual tasks'. Bennett *et al.* (1984: 168) also found that children 'sat in groups but worked on independent tasks'.

Types of group

There are a number of possible approaches to group work, each of which has advantages and disadvantages. Bennett and Dunne (undated: 4) list the following:

- Children sit together but work individually for individual outcomes. The tasks do not demand cooperation but children may be influenced by discussion about them.
- Children work individually on elements of a task for a joint outcome such as the production of a group story or newspaper or the making of a set of objects as in a mathematics activity. This requires a certain amount of cooperation.
- Children work jointly on a task for a joint outcome or discuss a topic together.

93

They found in studying the groups that 'It is clear that children in collaborative settings demonstrate much greater involvement in their work, the amount of task-related talk being 22 per cent higher.'

Bennett (1985: 107) describes a number of types of group activity which have been tried here and in the USA:

- *Team-games tournament* Children are placed in mixed teams of four or five. 'Following a class lesson the teams (groups) are given work sheets on which they work together and quiz each other to make sure the material is understood. At the end of the week a tournament is held, at which individuals represent their team in competition with individual representatives of the other teams. Team points are awarded on the basis of the individual's performance.' This is an idea put forward by Slavin (1990: 228) who suggests that 'The idea behind this form of cooperative learning is that if pupils want to succeed as a team, they will encourage their team mates to excel and will help them to do so. Often pupils do an outstanding job of explaining difficult ideas to one another by translating the teacher's language into their own.'
- *Jigsaw* Children work in mixed teams but the tasks are given in sections and each team member studies one section with members of other teams who have been allocated the same section. 'They then return to their own group and teach the section to the other group members. Finally all group members are quizzed on all sections of the task.'
- *Group investigation* An area of work is selected by the teacher, and children in small groups select sub-topics within the area. The groups divide the sub-topics into tasks for each member which are studied in preparation for a group presentation to the whole class.
- *Paired work* There are many situations in which paired work can succeed. Pairs can work together at tasks and problems or one member can tutor the other. Paired work is a good starting point for group work. Millard (1994) suggests that children might discuss in pairs stories they have written, commenting on what they liked or found interesting in each other's stories and whether there was anything in the story that they wanted to know more about. They could also correct each other's work.

Composition of groups

The composition of a group is an important element in its success. We saw in the last chapter that friendship groups are not always the most successful groups and do not give children the opportunity to work with a variety of different people. Dunne and Bennett (1990: 22) found that both high- and low-attainers worked well in mixed ability groups. Groups of high-attainers also worked well but groups of low-attainers did not. 'This seemed to be mainly because of a lack of understanding of the task – even combined group efforts failed to sort out problems. In addition, low-attaining pupils were not drawn into the task in the same way as when working in a mixed ability group.'

They found that 'high attainers not only do well in high ability groups. They do well in whichever kind of group they find themselves. They are of particular value in mixed ability groups where they are able to support their lower attaining classmates with inputs of knowledge, as well as suggestions and explanations' (p. 23).

It is helpful to consider personalities when forming groups. Some children naturally take the lead and these need to be distributed among the groups. Other children prefer to take a back seat. There will also be those who are helpful in a group at making its members keep to the point and work at the task in hand and others who distract the group.

Bennett and Dunne (1992) report that evidence is mixed about mixed gender groups. Teachers in their study found that infants worked well in mixed groups and through much of the junior school but negative views tended to develop as children grew older. Galton and Patrick (1990: 82) found that 'Single sex pairs and groups tended to do a little less than mixed pairs and groups, especially if individual tasks were assigned.'

Roles in group work

Biott (1987: 11) suggests that it is useful to identify the roles of group members. He gives the following examples:

- Encouraging and supporting others especially weaker members.
- Holding the group together in difficult moments.
- Questioning others to invite participation.
- Expressing doubts in a way which invites others to comment.
- Trying to express a half-formulated idea in a way which encourages others to join.
- Summarising progress in a tentative way and slowing the pace to make the group more reflective or speeding it up to test more ideas.

Galton and Williamson (1992: 143) suggest that:

Pupils should consider a range of roles, in addition to that of leadership, including helping to identify goals, summarising viewpoints, acting as 'willing followers' (who carry out the tedious tasks such as tidying up and generally keeping things going), helping to resolve disputes and focusing the discussion when it wanders from the point.

They suggest that the leadership role involves organising the task, defining goals, setting targets, allocating work, summarising and pressing for conclusion.

Bennett and Dunne (1992: 147) quote Johnson and Johnson (1985) who suggest that children can be allocated to specific roles within the group. The key roles might include:

- coordinator: to keep the group on task, to ensure contributions from all, to guide discussion or activity;
- data gatherer: to take notes or summarise ideas, to clarify ideas and to read aloud from some materials when appropriate;
- secretary: to record group answers or materials, spokesperson when reporting to the class;
- evaluation: to keep notes on the group process – how well individuals in the group are working together; to lead any evaluation at the end of the session.

The teacher has a difficult role during group work. You need to be monitoring the work of the groups but there may be an expectation on the part of the children that you will take over rather than listen. Delamont (1987: 39) found that children resented any takeover. She quotes a child who comments 'You have put all that work into it and then the teacher suddenly changes it.' Another child comments 'There are other times when they want to help us develop our own ideas and we are not certain when they come to see us which one is which' (p. 40).

This ambiguity probably accounts for the fact that Galton and Williamson (1992: 74) found that group work was disliked by children. Children in their study said 'that they had no way of knowing when a teacher was going to respond positively to what they were doing in groups'. They found that 'pupils claimed that they never knew where they were with teachers, that one minute everything was all right and the next "they were shouting at you"' (p. 112). The children showed a strong dislike of discussion and a preference for practical tasks. This was probably because both purpose and outcome were clearer in practical tasks and when they discussed ideas they did not know whether these would be acceptable to the teacher.

This suggests that you need to be very careful in how you manage group work. There is much to be said for not joining in the discussion if it is going reasonably well and making it clear to the children that you are simply listening to them and that you really want and value their ideas. Galton and Williamson quote one teacher as saying 'I am particularly conscious of that just now because I have spent a lot of time trying to stand back, watching and trying not to say trivial things like "That's nice" or "That's good"' (p. 107).

Group tasks

You need to consider carefully the types of task you provide for group work. Different types of task will lead to different types of discussion and involvement. Bennett and Dunne (1992) suggest that there are three main types of task:

- discussion where the work is to share understanding and ideas;
- problem solving where there is discussion of alternatives; and
- production tasks where there is a concrete outcome.

They suggest that simply asking children to discuss a topic is not very productive. It may be better to give children a series of statements and ask them to decide which they agree with or a number of questions to consider. They note that 'It is the need for decision making that focuses the children's responses' (p. 75).

There are considerable advantages in starting group work with a practical task since children find this easier to do than more abstract tasks which can be tackled later when children have learned how to work in a group. Bennett and Dunne note that teachers need to train children in planning an investigation, making it clear that they need to plan before starting to take action.

Possible tasks might include such things as working out how to make cuboids of different sizes from a flat sheet of paper, turning a story read together into a newspaper article, finding out which things float and which sink, arranging a collection of cut up sentences or pictures to form a story, working out what should fill the blanks in cloze procedure and so on.

Galton and Williamson (1992: 153) give the following check-list drawn up by teachers to help them to decide on the suitability of a task for groups of children who were new to working collaboratively:

Does the task:
1 Provide each child with an opportunity to be physically involved (e.g. handling apparatus).
2 Give an opportunity for each child to take part actively (e.g. in making a verbal contribution).
3 Involve only skills of which the children already have some understanding.
4 Have a definite objective so that the children know when they have finished.
5 Require the children to work in a way that it would be difficult for one child to complete the activity alone.
6 Offer a structure so that there is a definite logical progression of stages.

7 Have a clearly laid out set of instructions.
8 Have the appropriate equipment and resources readily to hand.
9 Lend itself to being done in a normal classroom situation (time, space and noise).
10 Allow for the minimum need for teacher support or intervention initially.

Bennett and Dunne (1992) also suggest that it works better if all groups have the same task. The teachers in their study found that group work with computers tended to lead to discussion about what to do rather than about the topic being discussed.

They also studied the kind of talk which went on in group work. They found that the talk became more abstract when it was no longer related to the activity of the moment but was concerned with finding an explanation, reconstructing a story or a memory, discussing the order of events or the truth of a tale. Task related talk was highest in technology and lowest in language work but there was more abstract talk in language work.

When groups have finished their work there is often a case for sharing their findings with the class and presentation can become the required outcome of group work. Feedback to the class can be rather tedious and long drawn out, particularly if the groups are small. Reid *et al.* (1987) suggest that if children work in groups of four, a pair from one group can join a pair from another group and feedback their findings.

Evaluation

Group work needs to be evaluated from two points of view. You need first of all to be concerned with what the children are actually learning from the topic under consideration. Secondly you need to be concerned with whether they are learning the skills needed to work in a group. It can be helpful to tape some sessions so that you can listen to the tapes after the lesson and consider how well the children were doing. It may also be helpful in training the children in group work to play back some parts of a tape which demonstrate children showing particular skills such as building on what someone else has said, summing up the findings of the group or encouraging other people. You need to be very clear in your own mind about the skills involved in working in a group so that you can identify how well the children are doing and help them to develop the necessary skills.

Bennett and Dunne (1992: 194) suggest that teachers need to consider the following questions about evaluation:

● what are you going to assess?
● how are you going to assess it?

- how are you going to feedback to pupils and groups?
- how are you going to record your assessment?
- how are you going to use this information in planning future tasks?

Children also need to be involved in evaluating both the extent to which they achieved the task and the way the group worked. If they are to do this, you need to make clear to them the skills you are wanting them to develop. A group work session might conclude with the groups considering how well they have done both in achieving the task and working as a group. Galton and Williamson (1992: 168) give a list of questions which a group might be asked to discuss.

Communication   *Yes*   *No*
1 Did all group members feel free to talk?
2 Was there any interrupting or cutting off?
3 Did people listen to one another?
4 Were group members asked to expand a point they were trying to make?

Participation
5 Did all members have opportunities to share their ideas?
6 Did any member(s) dominate?
7 Were group members sensitive to the needs and concerns of other group members?

Decision making
8 Did the group consider a number of ideas before coming to a conclusion?
9 Did everyone agree to the decisions that were made?
10 Was there any organisation in the group?

Conclusions

Group work is not an easy option for you or for the children. It requires careful planning both by you as the teacher and in the groups, and children need to be trained in the skills involved. When it is well done it can save your time and children learn a valuable way of working which is needed in many walks of life.

Webb and Vulliamy (1996: 39) make the following suggestions about getting started:

- Introduce small group work gradually by starting with children working in pairs.

- Initially keep group tasks relatively short and straightforward, such as brainstorming lists, predicting the end of a story and playing number games with calculators.
- Explain to the pupils exactly what is expected of them in group work. Ask them to draw on their early experiences to suggest some rules to guide the conduct of group work.
- Make sure the task is adequately resourced, with notional time allocation for different parts of the task and that pupils are clear about how they should go about achieving the intended outcomes.
- Ensure that everyone has a job to do and is actively involved in contributing to the group task.
- Tape-record group work to find out exactly what is going on in the groups and use pupil self-reflection to inform your evaluation.
- Enlist other audiences for the outcomes of group work – peers, other classes, parents and visitors – to give the task more status and to provide additional feedback.

9

THE TEACHING OF LITERACY

The Bullock Report (DES 1975: 7) made the following statement about the teaching of English:

> English is rooted in the processing of experience through language. The pupil uses language to represent the experience to himself, to come to terms with it, to possess it more completely. It is a major part of the teacher's skills to extend the range of that experience, at first hand and through literature, in such a way that new demands are made on language.

The National Literacy Strategy (DfEE 1998a: 3) lists the following skills which should be possessed by literate children. They should:

- read and write with confidence, fluency and understanding;
- be able to orchestrate a full range of reading cues (phonic, graphic, syntactic, contextual) to monitor their reading and correct their own mistakes;
- understand the sound and spelling system and use this to read and spell accurately;
- have fluent and legible handwriting;
- have an interest in words and their meanings, and a growing vocabulary;
- know, understand and be able to write in a range of genres in fiction and poetry, and understand and be familiar with some of the ways in which narratives are structured through basic literary ideas of setting, character and plot;
- understand, use and be able to write a range of non-fiction texts;
- plan, draft, revise and edit their own writing;
- have a suitable technical vocabulary through which to understand and discuss their reading and writing;
- be interested in books, read with enjoyment and evaluate and justify their preferences;

- through reading and writing, develop their powers of imagination, inventiveness and critical awareness.

The literacy hour is now being implemented in schools and gives teachers a clear picture of how to set about literacy teaching. It is intended to be an interactive period where children make considerable contributions to the work in hand. Medwell *et al.* (1998) who carried out a study of effective teachers of reading found that they made a point of stressing the literacy focus of the lesson to children at the outset. The literacy strategy should help teachers to be able to do this.

The National Literacy Trust paper (1998: 6), written for governors, says that schools should now have a literacy policy which:

- makes it clear that everyone in the school community can contribute to improving literacy;
- includes targets for improvements in literacy standards;
- promotes consistency in marking work, checking presentation, spelling and handwriting;
- includes a development plan to stimulate interest and enthusiasm for reading;
- provides strategies for working with pupils who have reading difficulties;
- uses Information and Communication Technologies (ICT) to support literacy across the curriculum.

Speaking and listening

The National Curriculum for English (DES 1995: 2) states that:

To develop effective speaking and listening pupils should be taught to:

- use the vocabulary and grammar of standard English;
- formulate, clarify and express their ideas;
- adapt their speech to a widening range of circumstances and demands;
- listen, understand and respond appropriately to others.

Children start school with very varied language experience. Some will use standard English most of the time, others may use a local dialect or speak a different language at home. There will also be some children who speak very little even though they may be quite talkative at home. Teachers of young children will also have some children whose articulation is not clear. The task with all these children is to extend their use of language.

Young children need to talk themselves through their activities. Vygotsky (1978: 26, 27) suggests that 'Speech not only facilitates the child's effective manipulation of objects but also controls *the child's own behaviour.*' He goes on to say 'Functionally, egocentric speech is the basis for inner speech, while in its external form it is embedded in communicative speech.'

Teachers are very likely to feel that children who speak a local dialect are less intelligent than those who speak standard English. This may not necessarily be the case. Working-class children tend to be stereotyped by teachers and the language experience they have tends to be underestimated. A study by Tizard and Hughes (1984) of a group of thirty pre-school girls, fifteen from middle-class homes and fifteen with a working-class background, was described in Chapter 3. The researchers visited them at home and studied the language used and then studied them in nursery school classes. They found that all the children used language more, asked more questions and explored more topics at home than at school.

This study suggests that while there are differences among children according to social class, they are more complex than is sometimes assumed. The study found that there was a much smaller amount of adult/child talk at school even though the schools in question were nursery schools with a much better adult/child ratio than reception classes. School conversations were very brief – on average half as long as conversations at home. They were also more adult-dominated than home conversations. The children themselves asked fewer questions at school than at home. 'The girls asked their mothers on average twenty-six questions an hour at home, but they asked only two questions an hour of their teachers' (p. 200). A large proportion of the questions that were asked were about routines and the business of the classroom rather than questions of curiosity.

Wood *et al.* (1980), working with under fives, found that the teachers who asked the most questions had fewest questions asked of them, whereas teachers who talked to children about their own ideas and observations were likely to receive many more ideas and questions from the children.

Teachers of children just starting school need to give a good deal of attention to the language skills they arrive with. It may be a good idea to try to have an extended conversation with two or three children each day, using opportunities which arise and making other opportunities. Tough (1976: 34) describes this as a process of appraisal which 'in our view means building up a picture of a particular child, being able recognise what he is already able to do in using language and discovering what he may not yet be able to do by talking to him'.

She goes on to suggest some of the things which the teacher might look for:

● How far does the child rely on speech for making and maintaining relationships with others?

- How good is the child's production of speech? Does he or she articulate clearly? Is he or she able to apply the common rules of language such as the use of plurals and pronouns?
- What does he or she use speech for? Does he or she initiate conversation? Does he or she respond to others?

In some schools teachers will be faced with children who have very little English. It will be particularly important to assess the amount of English such children have at an early stage so that a programme for helping them to settle into school and learn English can be planned. Stevenson (1992) suggests that teachers need to assert the positive benefits of the child's first language to children and parents. She quotes evidence that children who speak other languages at home tend to perceive their first language negatively. 'Parents should understand the value of proficiency in the first language to gaining proficiency in the second language' (p. 34).

Morgan (1992: 37) states:

> We are now coming to understand that children are most likely to develop into confident talkers in a climate where they:
>
> - Feel able to make mistakes, speak tentatively and think ahead knowing they are not being judged.
> - Believe that their own language and way of speaking are respected and their opinions taken seriously.
> - Experience a physical environment and organisation of learning in schools which encourage collaborative talk and opportunities to develop this talk beyond the immediate task in hand.

An important part of learning to use spoken language as children grow older is a developing appreciation of the need to match the subject matter to the purpose and to match the audience. The English programme of study for the National Curriculum suggests that children should be given the opportunity to talk to groups of varying sizes 'including friends, the class, the teacher and other adults in the school' (p. 4). Group work is a particularly valuable opportunity for practising oral language and it is a good idea to tape group discussion from time to time as well as listening to groups at work in order to assess the types of language which the children are using and the involvement of different children in the group.

Sutton (1981) suggests the following ideas for group talk:

- Two things to compare and contrast listing similarities and differences, for example two maps of the same area, two newspaper stories, two pictures.

- Prediction using extracts from a story with gaps one or two sentences long. Children have to predict what the sentences said.
- Devising questions. Each group has to devise five questions on a topic they have studied and decide what would be good answers. Groups then exchange questions and try to answer the questions which another group has set.
- Imagining other people's point of view given a short description or a picture of a situation involving several people. The group have to describe how each person feels about the situation.

Listening is also developed in group work and it may help to discuss how you know that someone is actually listening to you. The listener may use eye contact, may lean towards the speaker or react to what is said by movement or facial expression.

Drama offers good opportunities to use speech and think about the way different people speak in different situations. Yates (1990: 128) suggests that:

> Through drama, children have opportunity to use language in role play to express ideas, arguments, feelings, and to select and use forms of language appropriate to the character and situation. This in turn can lead to the discussion of how we choose and use language, and the factors which affect those uses.

The National Curriculum explicitly states that children should be taught to use standard English. It suggests that children 'should be introduced to some of the features that distinguish standard English, including subject-verb agreement and the use of the verb "to be" in past and present tenses' (p. 5). It will be important to do this in a way which does not give children the idea that the way they speak at home is inferior. Standard English is important because it is common to all English speakers who may each have local dialects as well which may not be fully understood by other people. It may also be important for getting a job when they grow older. You also need to avoid making children self-conscious about the way they speak by correcting them when they have something which is important to them which they want to communicate. The teacher's task in developing skill in using standard English is a delicate one. Joan Tough (1973: 58) recommends that teachers choose 'a moment when the correction will not stem the flow of talk but will give rise to another kind of discussion'.

Opportunities for pupil talk are limited by the size of the class and the fact that if a child hesitates or says too much others may lose interest. French (1987: 75) found that at infant level about two-thirds of the speaking turns were taken by boys. 'Boys seemed to *capture* the teachers' attention more than girls, and also to *demand* their attention. Teachers responded by seeking to involve them in the lessons rather than allowing them to become uninterested and, possibly, disruptive.'

Reading

The ability to read is a fundamental skill which children need to acquire in the primary school. It is an essential basis for their future learning across the curriculum.

Medwell *at al*. (1998: 8, 9) studied the work of 228 teachers of reading. From these they selected twenty-six as highly effective, whom they interviewed and observed at work. They also selected a control group of teachers from whom they collected similar data. Their main findings were as follows. They found that effective teachers of literacy:

- Believe that it is important to make it explicit that the purpose of teaching literacy is enabling their pupils to create meaning using text.
- Centred much of their teaching of literacy around 'shared' texts, that is, texts which the teacher and children either read or wrote together.
- Teach aspects of reading and writing such as decoding and spelling in a systematic and highly structured way and also in a way that makes clear to pupils why these aspects are necessary and useful.
- Emphasise to their pupils the functions of what they were learning in literacy.
- Have developed strong and coherent personal philosophies about the teaching of literacy which guide their selection of teaching materials and approaches.
- Have well-developed systems for monitoring children's progress and needs in literacy and use this information to plan future teaching.
- Have extensive knowledge about literacy although not necessarily in a form which could be abstracted from the context of teaching it.
- Have had considerable experience of in-service activities in literacy, both as learners and, often, having themselves planned and led such activities for their colleagues.
- Be, or have been, the English subject coordinator for their schools.

They also found that the effective teachers of literacy were more likely than the control group to give a high priority to purpose, communication and composition and to connect work at the word level, sentence level and text level.

Beginning reading

There has been a good deal of discussion over the years about the best approach to beginning reading. Overall the conclusion seems to be that mixed methods are required. Children need to learn about sounds and how these come together to make words as well as looking for meaning. The National Curriculum makes it clear that phonic knowledge and contextual understanding are both essential parts of learning to read.

Young children in today's world are surrounded by print and most will have learned to recognise a few words which are important to them. Recognising print in the environment can be one of the first signs of emerging literacy skills. Miller (1996: 13) suggests that 'It is by putting repeated guesses to the test, that children come to have a meaning base for making sense of the written language around them.' She points out that children read the contextual clues of language in the environment rather than the print at the early stage. Nevertheless, schools can make use of this early knowledge, particularly in planning children's play where properties can be included which need written notices. Shops, post offices, a telephone pad can all be included and give experience of the use of writing to communicate.

There is evidence that children's ability to recognise rhyme can predict their progress in reading. Bryant and Bradley (1985) studied 400 children between the ages of 4 and 5 over a period of four years. The 4 year olds were in nursery school and the 5 year olds were in their first term at school. They tested the children at the beginning of the study to see how well they could recognise rhyming words. At the end of the study they gave the children final tests which 'measured how intelligent they were and how well they could read and spell and as an essential extra check, some mathematical problems' (p. 57). They found that:

> The children's score on the initial rhyming tests did predict their progress in reading and spelling three or four years later on, and did so very well. The relationship stood even when we removed the effects of difference in intelligence ... The children's early rhyming scores did not seem to bear any relation to their success in mathematics.
>
> (Bryant and Bradley 1985: 57)

They also worked with a group of sixty-five six-year-olds for two years, dividing them into four groups and giving three of the groups slightly different teaching about the sounds in words. One of the groups was taught about rhyme and alliteration using pictures of common objects. A second group made the connection with reading more explicit. The children were taught to identify the sounds which the names of the pictures had in common using plastic letters to form the words. The third group was taught to put pictures into conceptual groups. The fourth group was a control group which did not receive specific teaching.

They found that 'measures of children's sensitivity to rhyme and alliteration predict their progress in reading, and teaching about rhyme and alliteration enhances that progress' (p. 61). The children in the second group did better than those in the other groups, including group one.

Medwell *et al.* (1998) found that effective teachers of reading used teaching about phonics as a means to an end whereas in the control group 'phonics worksheets were heavily used but little attempt was made to help children apply the phonic blends they were learning to the reading of continuous texts' (p. 30). 'The effective teachers were more likely to spend time looking at letter sounds in the context of reading a big book or a text written by the teacher and to do short, regular, modelling sounds activities' (p. 33).

Frank Smith and Kenneth Goodman are widely known for advocating concentrating on reading texts rather than working with sounds. Goodman (1973: 23) describes reading as follows:

> The *receptive* reader does start with the phonological or graphic display as input, and it does end with meaning as output, but the efficient language user takes the most direct route and touches the fewest bases necessary to get to his goal. He accomplishes this by *sampling* relying on the redundancy of language, and his knowledge of linguistic constraints. He *predicts* structures, *tests* them against the semantic context which he builds up from the situation and the on-going discourse, and then *confirms* or disconfirms as he processes further language.

Smith (1978: 56) points out that 'phonics works if you know what a word is likely to be in the first place' and suggests that 'The two best clues to any word are its total context – the meaning in which it is embedded – and its similarity to words that are already known' (p. 67).

The work of Smith and Goodman leads naturally to the 'real books' approach. Blackburn (1986) describes work by Cummins and Swain (1986) with two groups of bilingual reception class children one of which used a reading scheme with teaching about phonics and the other a 'real books' approach. They found that on grapho-phonic miscue the reading scheme children did better. They looked more closely at words and had a core vocabulary. The story book children were still memorising text. However, the story book children were better at supplying words which were correct for meaning when they tackled an unknown word but by a smaller margin. There were children in both groups who had difficulty.

The National Curriculum states that children 'should be shown how to use their knowledge of word order and the structure of written language to confirm or check meaning' (p. 7). It also stresses 'focusing on meaning derived from the text as a whole' and lists ways in which children should be encouraged to respond to stories and poems.

Smith (1978) points out that reading involves prediction about what is coming and some early reading books tend to be written in somewhat unnatural language which makes the task of prediction difficult. This is something to look out for in choosing books. Children are helped to learn to predict by listening to stories which will make the narrative style familiar so that they can more easily predict what is coming.

The Bullock Report (DES 1975: 92) states that 'The most effective teaching of reading . . . is that which gives the pupil the various skills he needs to make the fullest possible use of *context cues* in searching for meaning.'

It is important at the early stages of reading to ensure that children understand the language of instruction. Do they know the special use of the word 'letter' as it occurs in learning to read? Do they know what a word or a sentence is? Do they understand the words 'sound' and 'rhyme'? You need to check these points with individual children so that you are sure that they are understanding what you are saying about reading and writing.

Hearing reading

There are two important reasons for hearing reading. In the first place children need to practise reading and this means that they need as many opportunities as possible to read to someone who can prompt them if they falter. Almost anyone who can read can help with practice reading and schools need to make as much use as possible of parents and older children as listeners. Secondly as the teacher you need to hear children read in order to assess how they are doing. Can they build words from sounds? Do they understand what they are reading? Can they predict what is coming next? Hearing reading is also an opportunity to correct mistakes, to teach new skills and to check whether children are reading books at the appropriate level. Southgate *et al.* (1981: 109) give the following ranges of achievement:

Reading level	Word recognition	Comprehension
Independent	99–100 per cent	90–100 per cent
Instructional	95–98 per cent	70–89 per cent
Frustration	less than 95 per cent	less than 70 per cent

Southgate *et al.* studied over a thousand children and their teachers. They looked at the ability of teachers to assess children's reading performance and compared the teachers' estimates with test performance. They found that while nearly 36 per cent of the children's performances were underestimated by more than three months, only 28 per cent were overestimated by this amount' (p. 95).

There have been a number of studies of involving parents in hearing children read, all of which have demonstrated good progress resulting from this. Topping and Wolfendale (1985: 12) describe the contributions teachers and parents make to children's developing skill in reading as follows:

Teachers bring knowledge of child development and of theories of learning and teaching and have the advantage of an accumulating store of professional wisdom as the backcloth to their practice. They can appraise individual differences in learning receptivity, rate of learning etc. and can match each child's learning needs to the provision on offer.

Parents contribute their life experience as well as accumulating knowledge of their own child's (or children's) development and individual characteristics and have the advantage of experiencing minute by minute child contact in a variety of situations. They too, can appraise their child's responsiveness; they can make predictions as to outcomes and make a match between what the child needs . . . with whatever resources and support the home has to offer.

Various approaches have been tried involving parents or other tutors in hearing reading. Hewison (1985: 45) describes research in Dagenham which found that 'Children whose parents heard them read regularly tended to be much better readers than those whose parents did not.' The study also found that: 'When the pattern of reading scores across the different groups was studied, it emerged that children in homes where the language atmosphere was apparently unfavourable, but where help with reading *was* given, still tended to be better readers.'

Topping (1985: 109) describes 'paired reading'. This is a situation in which parent and child read aloud together adjusting the pace to what the child can manage. Errors are corrected by the parent giving an example and getting the child to repeat the word. When the child feels confident enough to continue reading alone, he or she gives a signal. The parent praises the child for this and for self-corrections and deals with errors as before by modelling the correct word. This approach has been found successful in the schools where it has been tried. Carrick-Smith (1985: 150) describes a study in which the overall gains for paired reading were twice that of the control group. He also reports that: 'Parents reported all manner of benefits, not only in reading skills, but in behaviour and personal relationships, even in the few cases where radical improvements in scores did not occur.' Parents are also reported to need some training in using the approach, particularly in the need to praise.

Another approach is called 'Pause, prompt and praise'. Topping (p. 166) describes how this approach deals with the situation when a child is 'stuck' for a word or makes an error:

Parents are asked to pause to allow self-correction, and if this does not occur to make a tripartite discrimination as to the nature of the error made. If the mistake makes no sense, the parent prompts the child with clues about the meaning of the story. If the mistake does make sense, the parent prompts with clues about the way the word looks. If the child stops and says nothing, the parent prompts by asking the child to read on to the end of the sentence (to search for contextual clues). If the error word is not correctly read after two prompts the parent tells the child what the word is.

Each time the child succeeds in correcting the error he or she is praised.

Wheldall and Glynn (1989) describe a study in which pause, prompt and praise was used with a group of older children tutoring low progress younger readers. Three groups for tutoring were set up. One group had tutors trained in pause, prompt and praise, one had untrained tutors and one was a control group. The younger children were tutored for six weeks with three thirty minute sessions each week. They were tested at the beginning and the end of the tutoring with a two month gap between the tests.

The children with the trained tutors made a mean gain of 6.2 months for reading accuracy. The untrained tutor group gained three months and the control group two months.

Docking (1990a: 155) summarises the benefits of involving parents which research has found:

1 Parents can substantially boost the time which children spend reading to adults. . . . Southgate *et al.* (1981) found that teachers gave an average of only two to three minutes per child per day. Parental involvement should not mean that teachers spend less time on reading, but rather that they use their time more effectively, perhaps developing more sophisticated approaches.

2 Children's interest in reading is likely to increase, as is the range and quantity of reading matter attempted.

3 Children are also more likely to be highly motivated towards school learning in general and behaviour is consequently better.

4 Relationships between parents and teachers are enhanced, and parents who formerly had remained distant from the school's effort to involve them usually take the opportunity to become more directly involved in their children's learning.

5 Parents and children develop closer relationships as the parents become more knowledgeable about their children's education, while children benefit from their parents' undivided attention for a short period each day.

Schools in which there are large numbers of children for whom English is a second language may need to look at other ways of providing extra help with hearing reading. One possibility in a primary school is to use older children. It may also be possible for older siblings of children to hear their reading at home. Some parents or governors may be prepared to come into school to hear reading. Jungnitz (1985), writing of work on hearing reading with Asian families, notes that one school not only used older siblings but also used tape-recorded stories for paired reading.

Advanced reading skills

The Bullock Report (DES 1975: 115, para. 8.2) gives three basic objectives for reading at the later stages of education which includes the older children in the primary school. These are:

- the pupil needs to be able to cope with the reading required in each area of the curriculum;
- he should acquire a level of competence which will enable him to meet his needs as an adult in society when he leaves school;
- he should regard reading as a source of pleasure and personal development which will continue to be a rewarding activity throughout life.

Bussis *et al.* (1985: 110) make the point that 'The skill of reading is an enabling skill, allowing access to a world of experiences far beyond the perceived realities of one's immediate surroundings.'

D'Arcy (1973: 79) describes the contribution of literature as follows:

If the refinement of our social responses is to depend to some extent at any rate upon the sharpening of our insights through literature, then the encouragement that we give to children to read books must be seen not simply as a way of influencing their leisure pursuits but, more fundamentally, as a way of influencing their development as human beings.

It is important to continue to read to children as they grow older. It is often a good way of introducing the work of a particular author whom you think some of the children will enjoy. It is also a way of introducing different genres of writing and particularly a way of giving children insight into books which may be a little too difficult for them to read independently. There should also be many opportunities to discuss books, stories and poetry, both as a class and individually. There is also a place for group discussion of reading. Groups can discuss how they think a story will work out, given the beginning or what a story had been about given an ending and their reasons for their views in each case.

Group reading in which children in small groups take turns in reading aloud from a book can give good practice in reading and provides an opportunity for children to help each other. Groups need to be of roughly similar ability and the books matched to the groups.

Children need to be helped to read non-fiction profitably. They need first to learn how to find the books they need from the class or school library using catalogues, indexes and contents lists. The Literacy Hour may include reading of science, history or geography texts. They need to learn to use dictionaries and reference books. They need reading habits which will enable them to obtain information from non-fiction texts. They need the ability to skim a text to get the general impression of what it is about and then to scan it for the detail which they need for the work in hand. They need practice in identifying the key points in a text and this leads to the development of skill in note-making. One way of doing this is to take a piece of text and get children to underline the words which are essential to the meaning. It can also be helpful to make a diagram of the key points linking them by arrows and lines.

Reid and Bentley (1996: 47) suggest that when children read non-fiction they need to know what kind of text they are reading and know also what they are expected to recall after reading and what they are to do with the information. They list the following non-fiction genre:

Recount	A story-like genre – diaries, journals.
Report	Factual information is given but not explained – atlases, dictionaries, maps, diagrams.
Procedure	Instructions for an activity – instructions, directions, rules, recipes.
Explanation	Explaining why something happened – natural or social process of how something works.
Exposition	Persuasion – advertising, brochures, argument.
Discussion	Presenting different points of view – reports containing recommendations.

The different genres have different layouts and language structures and children need to become familiar with them. Non-fiction is generally written in the present tense as distinct from fiction which is more usually written in the past tense.

The reading environment

The classroom environment should offer many incentives to reading. Books should be well displayed and relevant books included in displays about topic work. There is much to be said for finding a time each day or at least several times a week when everyone reads, including the teacher.

Teachers need to consider how much time is actually spent by children in reading. Southgate *et al.* (1981: 137) studied teachers listening to children reading and found that 'the average time spent in total concentration on a child's oral reading was only thirty seconds'. They also noted that 'only rarely was it observed that a teacher asked either a direct or open-ended question of a child on the content of his oral reading'. There were also frequent interruptions when teachers were hearing children read.

Teachers need to consider how much time individual children actually spend in reading altogether. Millard (1994: 49) makes the point that 'Reading needs to be seen as an important part of the curriculum and not something to fill in time when other work has been completed, or as a quiet activity at the end of the day.' While it is reasonable to use reading to fill in time when other work has been completed it must be remembered that the children who need most practice are those most likely to be slow in finishing work.

Boys and girls tend to respond differently to the process of learning to read, with boys doing less well than girls at all stages. The National Literacy Trust paper on literacy (1998: 14) notes that 'In 1997 30 per cent of seven-year-old girls reached National Curriculum Level 3 in reading compared with just 23 per cent of boys. At eleven, 69 per cent of girls but 57 per cent of boys reached Level 4 in English.' Docking (1990b: 139) had similar findings. He also found that 'There was no evidence of a significant closing of the gap in reading achievement during the junior years.' Millard (1994: 97) found that in Year 7 twice the number of boys compared with girls described learning to read as hard. She also found that girls generally preferred reading fiction and boys non-fiction and 'The reading that boys select for themselves includes far more information and non-narrative materials than that chosen by girls.'

Evaluation of reading

As teacher you should be continually assessing children's skill in reading. Medwell et al. (1998) found that the effective teachers of reading made a greater use of miscue analysis and observation of children than the validation group and were less likely to use standardised tests. Twenty per cent used reading conferences. They also tended to observe and make notes about particular children covering the class over a period. They noted pupils' enjoyment of group and individual reading and discussed reading diaries with children.

Millard (1994: 175) suggests that teachers might keep portfolios of individual reading which might include:

- teacher's log of observations in different contexts e.g. when children read their own work to others;
- systematic records of pupil/teacher reading conferences;
- samples of passages selected for reading aloud to other children, parents or teachers, with comments;
- a comments book or journals shared by teacher, parents and reader;

- children's own records of the books they have read;
- children's reviews of particular genres of writing e.g. poetry and non-fiction as well as stories.

She goes on to describe reading conferences where sufficient time is allowed for extended discussion of books chosen by the child. This gives an opportunity to check that the book is at a level that the child can read independently and not at a frustration level. Appropriate questions can enable the teacher to assess whether the child can make predictions, hypotheses and inferences about what is being read. Finally the teacher and child can discuss future reading and agree targets.

Monk and Karavis (1996: 137) stress the importance of noting the approaches and strategies each child uses for learning and of encouraging child to reflect on him or herself as a learner. They suggest that it is helpful to plan to concentrate on a small number of children each day and observe them closely. Some of this observation may be in the context of group work.

> A group discussion around a shared text, could provide evidence of the ability to read aloud, contribute to a discussion, build on the comments of others, pose pertinent questions, read beyond the literal, make links with others' reading and support opinions by referring to the text.

Writing

Hammond (1998) suggests that there are four fundamental purposes for writing – to express, to persuade, to entertain and to inform. Children need opportunities to write for all four of these purposes. The Assessment of Performance Unit (APU) (DES 1981: 85) in seeking measures of writing ability develops these purposes further and suggests that writing may be 'to describe, to narrate, to record, to report, to change the reader's mind/to persuade, to request, to explain/expound, to plan and to edit'. The report notes that 'in all of these tasks, variation in *audience* and in the writer's control over *form* was envisaged'.

Learning to write for specific audiences should be part of the learning process from the beginning. It is very easy for children to see their writing as written for the teacher every time and you need to look for other audiences. Some of these will be imaginary audiences but wherever possible there should be opportunities to write for a genuine readership so that the effectiveness of the writing stands by the way it is received. Writing can sometimes be for parents. Different classes in the same school or different schools can write to each other. Older children can write stories for younger children. One school which had set up a post box at Christmas time continued to use it after Christmas for children to write for each other, which they were allowed to do at odd moments in the day. This gave rise to a lot of enthusiastic writing and children who normally wrote very little were encouraged to write in order to receive letters from other children.

Children may also write stories which they can staple into booklets for other children to read. Some may like to write about something they know how to do for others who may like to do it too and in this case the proof of the effectiveness of the writing is whether the explanation is good enough for the reader to carry out the same task as the writer.

Writing also needs to be in an appropriate form for its purpose. Children should gradually learn to write in different styles such as narrative, description, account of experiences, diary, review, newspaper stories, instructions and many others. Different styles can be introduced through their reading and the characteristics of each can be discussed. Many opportunities for writing in different styles arise through work in other subjects. Children need gradually to learn ways of describing scientific experiments and field studies, and writing reviews and reports as well as the forms of writing which are part of their English work.

The advent of the computer for word-processing has made a difference to the way schools are able to treat children's writing. The fact that work can be changed and corrected as one goes along and that spelling can be checked, makes it possible for children who may find handwriting slow and cumbersome to produce good looking work with few mistakes. The computer should not be used just for final drafts but children given opportunities to write on it directly so that they benefit from the ease of drafting. Drafting and improving on the first draft should in any case be a regular part of children's writing as they grow older, whether this is done by hand or on the computer.

Handwriting

The existence of the computer does not make the need to learn to write well by hand superfluous. Children need to learn the skills of letter formation. These need to be taught as a skill and also practised in situations where the writing has a use. Children need to learn how to hold the writing tool, how to form each letter and its orientation. There is much to be said for teaching a letter form with a hook for later joining up. Schools which have done this have not found that children have any real difficulty in associating the written form with the printed form needed for reading and there is only a minor task later on to teach a different letter formation in order to develop cursive writing. In fact some of the children taught this letter formation start joining their writing of their own accord. It is a mistake to leave children using print script once they have developed fluency in writing. As soon as they are writing any substantial amount they need to be taught cursive letter forms if they have not learnt these earlier.

Handwriting needs practice in its own right as well as being practised in the process of writing for other purposes. The school needs a handwriting policy and an agreed letter formation which all teachers encourage children to use. Children may also have difficulty at the early stages in finding the right amount of pressure on the pencil, making appropriate spaces between words and getting the proportions of letters correct.

Spelling

English spelling is not easy because there are many exceptions to common spelling rules. Children need to learn to map speech sounds on to letters and groups. However, English spelling is more systematic than is some-times believed and there are many spelling rules which are rarely taught. For example, the letter 'j' is normally found only at the beginnings of words or words with a prefix like 'injure' or 'prejudice'. Otherwise the 'j' sound is spelled 'dge' as in bridge or dodge. We gradually learn this kind of rule without ever expressing it. It is a good idea to get children to try to deduce the more general spelling rules from looking at selected pieces of text or lists of words. For example, the rule about doubling the consonant in the middle of a word with a suffix when the vowel is short can be worked out from looking at words such as canned and caned, filling and filing.

The National Curriculum (DfE 1995: 9) states that pupils at Key Stage 1 should be taught to:

- write each letter of the alphabet;
- use their knowledge of sound-symbol relationships and phono-logical patterns;
- recognise and use simple spelling patterns;
- write common letter strings within familiar and common words;
- spell commonly occurring simple words;
- spell words with common prefixes and suffixes.

At Key Stage 2 pupils should be taught to:

- spell complex, polysyllabic words that conform to regular patterns, and to break long and complex words into more manageable units, by using their knowledge of meaning and word structures;
- memorise the visual patterns of words, including those that are irregular;
- recognise silent letters;
- use the apostrophe to spell shortened forms of words;
- use appropriate terminology, including vowel and consonant.

(DfE 1995: 16)

Medwell *et al.* (1998: 27) found that effective teachers of literacy 'were less likely to rate favourably the teaching of spelling through spelling lists and more likely to value children helping each other to revise their writing'. However, these teachers were said to 'Teach aspects of reading and writing such as decoding and spelling in a systematic and highly structured way and also in a way that made it clear to pupils why these aspects were necessary and useful' (p. 8). They also taught both spelling and grammar in context wherever possible. They were likely to discuss letter sounds in the context of reading a big book.

Millard (1994: 26) notes that 'Good habits of spelling are encouraged by helping the child to form a visual image of the new word, rather than through spelling it out.' A useful way of learning spellings is to look at a word, trying to make a picture of it in the mind, cover it up and try to write it. The next step is to see whether the word was written correctly going through the same procedure again if it was incorrect. Children need to study the common phonemes of English in the context of writing as well as reading, looking at letter strings and words which have common spelling elements. It is often helpful to collect the spelling errors a child makes and try to discover the thinking that led to the error.

Grammar and punctuation

Medwell *et al.* (1998: 28) found that effective teachers of literacy taught grammar through texts. 'The children in their classes were often asked to deduce grammatical rules from presented extracts of language, often taken from shared texts.'

Work on texts can also include study of the functions of words in the text. The basic grammatical terms can be introduced and children can practise finding verbs, adjectives, nouns, adverbs and conjunctions.

Children and many adults have difficulty in using the apostrophe to show ownership. It can be helpful to explain that the phrase 'John's book' can be thought of as a contraction for 'John, his book' and is a similar idea to the contractions of 'can't' and 'don't' where the apostrophe stands for letters missed out. Of course this doesn't work when the phrase is 'Anne, her book' or 'the boys, their books' but it is a useful way of helping children to remember when to use the apostrophe.

Children take time to learn to punctuate sentences with commas and full stops. It can be useful to get them to listen to you reading and to put up their hands when you pause for a full stop. They need to get into the habit of listening in their heads to what they are writing so that they recognise when pauses come. They can also read their work aloud to each other and listen for where the full stops come.

Learning to write direct speech is difficult for many children. With older ones writing plays may be a way into this since it is only necessary to write the words which are to be said and the name of the person saying them. The text of a short play can then be turned into a story. Another approach is to study how direct speech is written in story books, getting children to work out rules for how you write this.

Narrative

Children start to write stories at an early stage and work can be done on helping them to recognise the demands of a narrative style. Narratives are usually written in the past tense and they need to start with some form of introduction to the scene and the characters. Children can discover this for themselves by looking together at stories. They can also work at describing characters and places in the story, looking at how different authors have done this. Next they need to recognise the plot of the story and in writing their own stories they need to work out the plot before they begin. Stories also offer a good opportunity for practising writing direct speech. It is helpful in writing book reviews if children are asked to write about setting, characters and plot.

Poetry

Many children enjoy writing poetry, especially if it can be accepted that it doesn't have to rhyme. They are more likely to be able to write poetry if they hear a lot of it and if poems are discussed and children are introduced to metaphor and simile in this context. Talking about how the poet made you see what he or she was talking about is something which can be discussed and children can be encouraged to try to do this for themselves. Writing each sentence on a new line is one way of leading into poetic writing which also helps children to recognise sentences.

Other forms of writing

Children need opportunities to write for many purposes so that they come to recognise the different styles of writing which are needed. Reports on work they have done, book reviews, writing instructions for someone else to carry out, diaries, newspaper reports and many other types of written work need to be included from quite an early stage. In each case it will be important to discuss the characteristics of the particular form of writing and how it differs from other forms. Children can then attempt their own versions. Discussion may be a class activity or it may be in pairs or small groups which report back to a class discussion.

10

THE TEACHING OF
MATHEMATICS

Knowledge of mathematics and skill in using numbers are essential for life in the modern world. At an elementary level we need to be able to count money for shopping and assess whether we are getting the right change. We need to to be able to work out calculations for household tasks like the cost of papering or carpeting a room. There are frequent references to amounts and quantities in newspaper articles and advertisements and we need a basic knowledge of statistics. At a more advanced level mathematics is an essential tool in many areas, for example physical science, engineering, geography and economics. It is a tool of communication. Adults in today's world need to be numerate. Although the development of calculators has changed the need for basic calculation it is still essential to understand the concepts behind the calculations in order to use the calculator effectively.

The National Numeracy Project *Framework for Numeracy* (1997: 4) gives the following definitions of numerate primary pupils. They should:

- have a sense of the size of a number and where it fits into the number system;
- know basic number facts and recall them quickly;
- use what they know to figure out an answer mentally;
- calculate accurately, both mentally and with pencil and paper, drawing on a range of strategies;
- recognise which operation is needed to solve a problem;
- be able to solve a problem involving more than one single step operation;
- know for themselves that their answers are reasonable;
- explain their methods and their reasoning using correct terminology;
- suggest suitable units for making measurements, and make sensible estimates of measurements;
- explain and make sensible predictions for the numerical data in a graph, chart or table.

Ofsted (1996: 4) found that 'The quality of teaching is satisfactory or better in about four-fifths of lessons in Key Stage 1 and good or very good in over one-third. . . . There remains, however, a lack of challenge and pace in a quarter of the schools at Key Stage 2, and teaching is more variable in Key Stage 2 than Key Stage 1.'

It found that at Key Stage 2 in particular, teachers tended to use published schemes inappropriately and excessively, and that 'this leads to a poor match of work to the full range of pupils' abilities and a lack of differentiation'.

Characteristics of effective teachers

Askew *et al.* (1997) studied the work of teachers of mathematics looking particularly at the characteristics of those teachers who were most effective. They categorised teachers into three orientations – the connectionist orientation, the transmission orientation and the discovery orientation.

They defined the connectionist orientation 'as including the belief that being numerate involves being both efficient and effective'. They found that connectionist teachers emphasised the links between different aspects of mathematics and encouraged pupils to 'draw on their mathematical understanding to solve realistic problems' (p. 27).

The transmissionist teachers demonstrated a belief in the importance of a collection of routines and procedures, and stressed the importance of pencil and paper methods for each type of calculation regardless of whether a different method might be more effective in a particular situation. They believed that word problems should be tackled after children had learned to do the calculations involved.

The discovery-orientated teachers tended to treat all methods of calculation as equally acceptable and valued pupils' creation of their own ways of doing things, basing work on practical approaches. They believed that 'learning about mathematical concepts precedes the ability to apply these concepts and application is introduced through practical problems' (p. 30).

Askew *et al.* also listed the characteristics of effective teachers of mathematics. These included the following:

- a coherent set of beliefs and understandings which underpinned their teaching of numeracy;
- a belief that being numerate requires having a rich network of connections between different mathematical ideas;
- a belief that almost all pupils could become numerate;
- a view that discussion of concepts and images was important, particularly in revealing the pupils' thinking processes;
- attention to careful monitoring of pupil's progress and the keeping of detailed records.

They also found that high effectiveness in teachers was not necessarily linked with having an A level or degree in mathematics but was linked with having experienced substantial in-service training over a period.

The characteristic which stands out most strongly in this study is the ability of the teachers concerned to demonstrate links between different aspects of mathematics. The connectionist teachers were more effective than the transmissionist teachers or those concerned with discovery whom the researchers found to be only moderately effective. The Cockcroft Report (DES 1982: 69) makes a similar point: 'Research evidence makes it clear that information is stored better in long-term memory if it is assimilated in such a way that it becomes part of a network of associated and related items which support one another.'

Teaching approaches

The National Numeracy Project *Framework for Numeracy* (1997: 5) describes the approach which was being used in the classes taking part in the pilot scheme of the project. There were three key principles laid down for them:

- regular lessons every day;
- a clear focus on direct, instructional teaching and interactive work with the whole class and groups;
- an emphasis on mental calculation.

The Project defines the broad areas of understanding, skills and knowledge to be taught as follows:

Knowledge of numbers and the number system
- counting
- properties of numbers and number sequences
- place value and ordering (including reading and writing numbers)
- estimating and rounding
- fractions, decimals and percentages, and their equivalence

Calculations
- understanding number operations
- quick mental recall of number facts
- mental calculation strategies, including strategies for deriving new facts from those already known
- pencil and paper methods
- checking that the results of calculations are reasonable

Making sense of numerical problems
- making decisions: deciding which operation and method of calculation to use (mental, part mental part pencil and paper, calculator, spreadsheet)

- reasoning about numbers and making general statements about them
- solving problems involving numbers in everyday life and other familiar contexts:
    involving money
    involving measures, including choosing units and reading scales
- handling numerical data

Rosenshine and Stevens (1986: 377) note that effective teachers used direct instruction. The effective teacher:

> begins the lesson with a short review of prerequisite learning . . . announces the goals of the lesson . . . presents new material in short steps . . . gives students practice in each step . . . gives clear and detailed explanations and instructions . . . gives a high level of inter-active and successful practice.

Desforges and Cockburn (1987: 7) note that a great deal of unsatisfactory mathematics teaching is rather like this. 'The teacher explained a mechanical procedure in the mathematics scheme and the children did pencil and paper exercises to practise the routine. Eighty per cent of mathematics teaching in our study conformed to this pattern.' They also say 'Extensive surveys of classroom practice indicate that far from encouraging young children's mathematical inventiveness, the vast majority of school teachers have children playing a passive-receptive role as learners.'

There has been a good deal of encouragement to teachers to return to a greater proportion of class teaching in mathematics and to move away from the individualised pattern which has been the norm in many classrooms. Askew et al. (1997: 93) found that both the effective teachers and the control group of teachers used a mixture of whole-class teaching, group and individual work. They concluded that 'The mathematical and pedagogical purposes behind particular classroom practices seem likely to be more important than the practices themselves in determining effectiveness.'

The important thing in whole-class work would seem to be that it should be interactive, with children playing an important part themselves and not passively listening to and accepting the words of the teacher. Discussion is important in mathematics both at a whole-class level and in small groups and pairs where children can be encouraged to share their thinking about how to solve the problems in hand. Desforges and Cockburn go on to suggest that:

> The crucial element is that in their mathematics education, children should be actively engaged in exploring mathematical techniques in the face of substantive problems. Techniques should be discussed

amongst teachers and pupils. Pupils should discuss ideas with their peers. Discussing should develop confidence in sharing and evaluating ideas. Problems should relate to real life issues meaningful to pupils.

(Desforges and Cockburn 1987: 9)

They found teachers responding in various ways to the problem of providing for the wide range of ability and attainment in most classes. Some teachers worked with the whole class demonstrating and leading discussion and then divided children into ability groups with each group having work on the same concept but at a different level. In some cases 'the low attainers did meet the same work cards as the high attainers but their route was frequently made simpler by the use of supplementary materials, additional explanations and more support for the task from the teacher' (p. 55).

They found that there was very little original contribution from the children. 'Children's comments were never more than a short phrase and were always under the instigation of the teacher. There was no child-to-child talk. Whilst many children made some response, contributions from the class were dominated by only a small fraction of the pupils' (p. 75). They were critical of what happened when practical work was introduced. 'Whilst practical work was evident, it played, by and large, only a supporting role to paper and pencil work. The children rarely tackled real problems in their mathematics or applied their thoughts to anything other than the procedures demanded by the teacher' (p. 79).

HMI (DES 1985d: 4) support the views implied by this criticism. They suggest that teachers should encourage children to find their own ways of working out problems even when there may be a more streamlined method which they can learn later. They give as an example 'pupils who can multiply by a single digit number might be challenged to find how to multiply by larger numbers'.

They have some useful comments on the place and quality of exposition in mathematics teaching:

> Successful exposition may take many different forms but the following are some of the qualities which should be present: it challenges and provokes the pupils to think; it is reactive to pupils' needs and so it exploits questioning techniques and discussion; it is used at different points in the process of learning and so, for example, it may take the form of pulling together a variety of activities in which the pupils have been engaged; and it uses a variety of stimuli.
>
> (DES 1985d: 38, para. 4.7)

They go on to make the following comments about organisation:

- pupils of all abilities should be able to achieve their potential;
- the organisation should ensure that all pupils may experience a full range of classroom approaches;
- opportunities should be provided to allow pupils to work independently, to engage in cooperative work and to pursue topics of interest in some depth.

(DES 1985d: 43, 44, para. 4.16)

Drummond (1993: 91) stresses the importance of teachers listening to pupils. 'Teachers who investigate . . . children's mathematical thinking, by listening to their pupils thinking aloud, explaining their calculations, very quickly discover that apparent errors in the written record of those calculations are often the result of systematic mathematical reasoning.'

Desforges and Cockburn (1987: 102) also stress the need for teachers to investigate the way children are thinking in order to diagnose their difficulties. They found that 'The teachers did not find out about the degree of match between the tasks and children's attainment because they did not conduct any detailed diagnostic work. If a child could do a task all was well; if not he was re-taught.' They noted that teachers were not trained in diagnostic work and even when they were, previous research (Bennett et al. 1984) showed that they found it extremely difficult partly because of the distraction of the rest of the class while attempting to conduct a diagnostic interview with one child.

One of the problems of teaching mathematics is that of linking the mathematical learning to children's everyday life. Ideally there should be a good deal of work on real-life problems. Desforges and Cockburn (1987: 35) note that this is more difficult than it appears. 'A real-life problem doesn't come from school. Thirty experiences cannot be brought into the classroom.' In practice teachers have to make the connections as best they can. One way of doing this is to use cross-curricular opportunities when possible.

Cross-curricular work

The non-statutory guidance given in the early version of the National Curriculum in Mathematics (DES 1989b: F1, F2) notes that 'In life, experiences do not come in separate packages with subject labels. As we explore the world around us and live our day-to-day lives, mathematical experiences present themselves alongside others.' The guidance therefore stresses incentives for schools to plan cross-curricular work in mathematics:

- they reflect the real world in which we live;
- they enable more efficient use of time to be planned for;

- the contribution of mathematics to other areas of the curriculum can be maximised;
- working in a variety of contexts helps pupils to learn.

(DES 1989b: F1, F2, para. 1.7)

HMI in the primary survey (DES 1978: 49) found that 'Techniques learned in mathematics were infrequently used in other areas of curriculum or related to everyday situations and children were seldom required to quantify as part of their recording except in mathematics lessons.' Although this survey is now a long time ago the message is still important. Teachers need to consider where in the curriculum they could introduce skills and concepts learned in mathematics lessons.

The non-statutory guidance cited above (DES 1989b: B11) suggests that activities should enable pupils to develop a positive attitude to mathematics and that attitudes to foster include:

- fascination with the subject;
- interest and motivation;
- pleasure and enjoyment from mathematical activities;
- appreciation of the power, purpose and relevance of mathematics;
- satisfaction from a sense of achievement;
- confidence in an ability to do mathematics at an appropriate level.

Language

Language plays an important part in mathematics. Children need to learn the particular use of mathematical words, especially where these are words in use in everyday situations but have more specific meanings in mathematical work. It is also important to remember that language needs to be linked to first-hand experience if it is to be understood and retained. Duffin (1987: 46, 47) makes the point that 'if children cannot talk to their teacher and each other, they cannot make progress in mathematics'. She lists the following suggestions about language in mathematics:

- Discussion is an important way to develop thought.
- Language development may be as important in mathematics as in other areas of the curriculum.
- Acquisition of spoken mathematical vocabulary may be useful in helping to read mathematics texts.
- Much mathematical language does not feature in the natural language of many people.
- Language coming out of activity provides a better way to develop mathematically than language built on to a mathematical process.

- Mathematics based on reality has more meaning for children than calculations presented out of context.
- Teachers need to listen to what children actually say rather than concentrating on their own perception of the correct answer to a question they have asked.

Calculators and computers

The use of calculators at the primary stage has generated a good deal of discussion. In practice it is impossible to ignore their existence in that many children will possess them or have access to them at home. It therefore seems sensible to find the most profitable ways of using them in schools.

While it is important that children learn to calculate without the aid of a calculator, the calculator makes it much more possible to use real-life problems that have numbers which can not easily be handled by children. It is also important to understand the concept underlying any calculation and calculators make this easier to do because children can do a number of calculations to discover patterns in a way which would be nearly impossible if the calculations had to be done with pencil and paper. Hughes (1987) suggests that children can use calculators in pairs with one child using the calculator and the other doing the calculation mentally, seeing which child is the quicker. He also notes that since division with a calculator does not lead to a remainder but to a decimal it provides a useful starting point for work on decimals. He suggests that estimation and checking should be an important part of work with calculators, with children undertaking the checks such as the following:

- Does the size of the answer make sense?
- Repeat the calculation in a different order.
- Roughly approximate – for example, is the decimal point in the right place?
- Use of pattern (32 × 17 should end in 4).
- Check that the input data are reasonable.
- Use the inverse process – for example, check subtraction by adding.

(Hughes 1987: 108)

The computer has the advantage of providing immediate feedback to the children using it. They know immediately if the sum they have done is right or wrong. There is also an advantage if children use the computers in pairs or small groups in that they can discuss the problems they find and experiment with the answers. Hughes (1987: 116) suggests that 'Good programs encourage mental arithmetic skills in a problem solving atmosphere, which also encourages vital discussion between pupils.'

Children can learn to use databases and spreadsheets and graphics programs and these offer opportunities for cross-curricular work. Computers offer good opportunities for following up practical work by tabulating, analysing and perhaps graphing results.

While it has been increasingly common for schools to invite parents to help children with reading by reading to them and hearing them read daily, it is less usual for parents to be invited to help with mathematics. Yet there is a strong case for looking for parental help, especially at the early stages. Parents have many opportunities in the home and neighbourhood to involve children in everyday uses of number, weight, capacity and area and it is worth taking time to suggest to parents ways in which they can support the work of the school, both by using opportunities which arise and also helping children to learn and remember number bonds and tables.

11

EXCEPTIONAL CHILDREN

All good teachers try to cater for all the children in the class but this is difficult, especially if the class is large and much of your class work has to be aimed at the average group. There will be some children, however, who need to be seen as exceptions. Some of them will be children with special educational needs who are slow learners, show behaviour difficulties or have physical problems. There will also be some who are far in advance of the rest of the class and have special needs of a different kind.

Identification and analysis

Your first task is to identify them. In most cases this is fairly easy. In any but the reception class previous teachers will have identified children with special needs and your special needs coordinator will have information about these children which will help you to plan work for them. In the reception class you may have information from a nursery school or play group but you will probably need to do a good deal of observing and checking using the baseline checks for children entering the school.

Children who are exceptionally able may be less obvious, especially as they grow older. Some will clearly stand out but there may be children who are deliberately slowing down so as not to seem different from their peers. There may also be working-class children with non-standard speech or children whose home language is not English whom it is easy to pass over. You need to be on the look out for those who are able but under-performing. Freeman (1998: 10) quotes research that suggests that teachers 'are good at selecting the high-level achievers, but had difficulty in identifying high-level intellectual and creative ability'. She also warns against stereotyping children and suggests that teachers should 'check that choices are not biased by social class, ethnicity, gender or handicap' (p. 11).

Freeman (pp. 12, 13) also gives the following check-list for identifying exceptionally able children:

- Memory and knowledge – excellent memory and use of information.
- Self-regulation – they know how they can learn best and can monitor their learning.
- Speed of thought – they may spend longer on planning but then reach decisions more speedily.
- Dealing with problems – they add to the information, spot what is irrelevant and get to the essentials more quickly.
- Flexibility – although their thinking is usually more organised than other children's, they can see and adopt alternative solutions to learning and problem-solving.
- Preference for complexity – they tend to make games and other tasks more complex to increase interest.
- They have an exceptional ability to concentrate at will and for long periods of time from a very early age.
- Early symbolic activity – they may speak, read and write very early.

There may also be exceptional children with specific gifts which will be revealed only if there is an opportunity. A child may have musical gifts but these will be apparent only if there is plenty of opportunity for making music. Exceptional leadership skills may reveal themselves in the playground as well as in the classroom but there needs to be scope for leadership for these to be seen. You need to be on the lookout for specific talents as well as general ability.

Identification of children with special needs, including the needs of the very able, should be followed by observation and analysis of the needs of the individual child. This is not easy in a large class but is possible if you are clear about the skills and characteristics you are looking for. In reading you need to check such things as the phonic knowledge a slow learner has. Does he or she understand the language used in talking about reading and writing, for example word, letter, sound, letter name? How many of the most common words can he or she read? In writing you need to check a child's ability to copy from a work card or the blackboard. Does the child form letters correctly? Can he or she use capital letters and full stops? The checks you make will depend on the age of the child but the important thing is to be clear about what you want to know and to keep a good record of your findings. Collecting the errors a child makes also provides clues to problems.

Similarly, in mathematics you need to check how each child is thinking. When he or she makes mistakes you need to question until you find out the thought processes which created the mistakes. You need to know how far the child knows the number bonds and later the multiplication tables and the extent to which he or she knows the routines for the various mathematical processes. Does the child understand the language you are using in mathematics?

In looking at the problems of slow learners you also need to check whether there are any physical problems. Can the child see and read what is on the board or in a book? Is his or her hearing adequate? Some children have difficulty in hearing particular sounds and you may get a clue about this from studying the mistakes made. You may also have a child who has problems in writing because of a physical disability or clumsiness. Left-handed children often find writing difficult because they tend to cover their writing with their writing hand. It is helpful if you encourage them to hold their book or paper at an angle so that this does not happen.

Lang (1990: 102) writes about disaffection in the primary school and suggests a number of starting points for studying children who pose behaviour problems. A teacher might look at the the state of the following in a child who is posing problems:

- Self-esteem: self acceptance and a healthy self-image
- Self-confidence
- Personal and social skills
- Responsibility
- Initiative: the ability to undertake and sustain independent effort
- Honesty/trust: the ability to express feelings honestly and openly to others
- Empathy
- Judgement: the ability to make appropriate decisions independently.

Winkley (1990: 82) writes of teachers who succeed with children who pose problems, possibly bringing those problems to school with them.

> They set about their professional task of trying to understand and then manage the child, admitting difficulties, but not externalising, not blaming the child, or covertly implying, as sometimes happens, that the child is there, in some way, to serve their own convenience. The teachers who succeed are above all determined to succeed, and are not unduly impeded by occasional failures.

He goes on to suggest that the teacher 'might begin by looking at basic management techniques, the use of rewards and sanctions and the role of feelings and insight in the teaching experience' (p. 82).

Welch (1990) suggests that inadequate identification of high potential and talent, coupled with poor provision, is a major cause of disaffection amongst the most able. Children who are under-extended will become bored and look for ways of making life interesting by causing disruption.

The Code of Practice for children with special needs (DES 1994: 24, para. 2.75) identifies information which should be part of the record for each child.

- class records, including any from other schools which the child has attended in the previous year;
- National Curriculum attainments;
- standardised test results or profiles;
- Records of Achievement;
- reports on the child in the school settings;
- observations about the child's behaviour.

Dean (1995: 36) adds the following to this list:

- check-lists which give specific information about what the child can and cannot do;
- collections of errors and miscue analysis which often clarify the nature of problems;
- notes of books, materials and approaches used and with what results;
- information about the child's attitudes to school and to learning;
- information about the child's confidence and self-esteem;
- information about attendance and particularly about absences;
- comment about the development of social skills.

In the case of children with physical disabilities the identification process will be a matter of discovering what the child can and cannot do and working out ways in which he or she can achieve. Writing may be a difficulty for some and it may help if they can learn to type at an early stage. You need to learn all you can about the nature of the disability and the ways in which you can help the child to cope in the classroom and get on good terms with his or her peers. Children with severe disabilities may have spent a lot of time in hospital and may need help in learning what makes them acceptable to other children, who, in turn, may need to be encouraged to involve the child with a disability in peer group activities. It is also important to be sufficiently demanding of such children. It is easy to make too many allowances for them and they need encouraging to do as much as possible in a similar way to other children.

Making provision

Hegarty et al. (1981: 431–3) concluded that for all children with special needs the school should specifically:

- have high expectations;
- give pupils responsibility;

- allow them to take risks;
- make a minimum of interventions;
- make concessions only when necessary;
- reduce excess dependence.

Another important element for all children, but especially those with special needs is the development of a positive self-image. Freeman (1979: 54) makes the following point:

> The single and longest lasting effect that a school has on its pupils is how it affects their self-concept. The whole system, but especially the teachers, has the potential to make or mar the way pupils think about themselves for life.

Provision for slow learners

When a child appears to have difficulty in learning your first task should be to check for physical problems. Can the child see the book he or she is using? Can he or she see the board? Is the child's hearing adequate? Does he or she lean the head to one side as if it is difficult to hear? You can test hearing by standing behind the child and whispering, asking for your words to be repeated. You can also look out for difficulty in hearing particular sounds. Many children have difficulty in distinguishing between 'f' and 'th'. Other sounds frequently confused by children with poor auditory discrimination are b and p, c and g, d and t. You can check whether a child can give the sounds for different letters and whether he or she can transcribe sounds. A child may also have difficulty in blending sounds. Spelling mistakes will often give clues to auditory difficulties. For example, a child may have difficulty with the final parts of words and may write such things as 'goll' for 'gold' or 'pich' for 'picture'. Similarly some children will have difficulty with the beginnings of words or may have a limited skill in recognising different vowels in the middle of words.

There is a good deal of evidence which suggests that intervention for children who appear to have learning difficulties needs to start early. Wolfendale and Bryans (1978: 3) note that failure is seldom reversible after the age of 8 or 9. They suggest that 'Early experience of failure on the part of the child, even minimal failure, seems to have a substantial negative effect which endures and reduces the benefits of remedial help.'

Sylva and Hurry (1995: 5) note that 'Research evidence points to the fact that, for reading difficulties, early intervention appears to be more effective than remediation at a later stage.' They also support the view that intervention needs to tackle a broad range of skills including explicit phonic instruction.

Clay (1972: 3) suggests that children who are not succeeding in reading by their sixth birthday need study and detailed teaching. She suggests that the teacher should make a diagnostic survey of the performance of such a child. It is desirable:

- to observe precisely what children are doing and saying;
- to use tasks that are close to the learning tasks of the classroom (rather than standardised tests);
- to observe what children have been able to learn (not what they have been unable to do);
- to discover what reading behaviours they should now be taught from an analysis of performance in reading, not from pictorial or puzzle material, or from normative scores;
- to shift the child's behaviour from less adequate to more adequate responding by training on tasks rather than training visual perception of auditory discrimination as separate activities.

She suggests that the teacher should check the following:

- Accuracy in book reading
- Letter identification
- Concepts about print
- A word test
- Writing vocabulary

In the work she did in New Zealand, children with reading difficulties are then taught individually by specially trained tutors in the Reading Recovery Scheme, which has also been successfully tried in Britain. Tansley and Panckhurst (1981: 255) describe a typical tutoring session as including the following:

- re-reading of two or more familiar books
- letter identification (plastic letters on a magnetic board)
- writing a story
- sound analysis of words
- cut-up story to be re-arranged
- new book introduced
- new book attempted.

The overall finding about Reading Recovery is that it is very effective in improving reading for children in difficulty in the short term and the effects are still evident at a later stage.

A number of schools have successfully adopted the practice of asking parents to hear children read. This was described in Chapter 9.

Among the children with difficulty in reading there may be some who are of average or above average intelligence but appear to have particular difficulty in learning to read and write. They may be suffering from dyslexia which Critchley and Critchley (1978: 149) describe as 'a learning disability which initially shows itself by erratic spelling and lack of facility in manipulating written as opposed to spoken words'. They suggest that this is not due to any intellectual inadequacy or emotional factors but may be a maturational defect.

Tansley and Panckhurst (1981) suggest that this type of problem may be helped by linking kinesthetic, auditory and visual information. Farnham-Diggory (1992) advises that such children need to acquire strategies for learning, such as how to break a task into manageable parts, how to monitor their own attention and how to distribute their study time. She suggests that phonograms are taught in isolation, four or five in each lesson, followed by extensive practice in their use so that they become automatic.

Montgomery (1990) suggests aiding the spelling of such children by helping them to see the roots of words or the parts that are alike and by tapping out the syllables. She also suggests that they are helped if they learn cursive writing from the beginning so that there is a flow.

Children with this kind of difficulty need to be given opportunities to produce work which is in accord with their intellectual level. It is helpful if a parent can type work at the child's dictation which he or she can later read back. The time will come when a child can dictate work to a computer and have it printed out. The computer is a valuable aid for children who find handwriting difficult. It enables them to produce work which is good looking and with the help of a spellchecker can be correct to a much greater extent than when they write by hand.

Children may also have difficulty in mathematics. Here the important task for the teacher is to find out how the child is thinking and thus to get to the root of the difficulty. Bennett *et al.* (1984) found that teachers were hesitant about trying to diagnose children's difficulties, preferring to re-teach rather than to explore the child's thinking. This is understandable given the pressures on teachers but it is only when a child realises that the process he or she is using is the cause of difficulty that progress can be made. At the same time it is important for such children to learn number facts very securely, practising them until they are well known.

Children with emotional or behavioural difficulties

Problems of behaviour are bound up with learning difficulties and some children misbehave because they are not succeeding in learning but are looking for other ways of making their presence felt. Some children with emotional and behavioural difficulties may have problems in their home background. Montgomery (1990: 130) summarises these as follows:

Home background can be seen as providing an 'at risk' factor by failing to supply the appropriate social techniques for fitting into a larger group, or it may fail to provide basic emotional support which the child then seeks to satisfy in various and often inappropriate ways in school.

Where families are under duress and there is discord and quarrelling, break-up and divorce, illness and hospitalisation, children again become vulnerable and there is anxiety and stress.

Knowledge of home background may make you sympathetic to a child but not every child from a broken home poses problems and not every child who poses problems comes from a home where there are problems. Your relationship with the child and his or her parents is important, particularly where there are difficulties at home. It is also important to remember that your main task is to help the child to learn.

Children with behaviour problems may not only have difficulty in conforming to the behaviour norms expected in school but may also have difficulty in getting on with their peers. You may need to spend time with them discussing social skills and helping them to see their actions from the point of view of other people. As children grow through the primary school they become increasingly more able to see from another person's point of view and this can be helped by literature and role play and drama.

Winkley (1990: 81) suggests that 'The underlying principles [for dealing with children with behaviour problems] are those of good parenting. Rewarding is essential; consistency, fairness and firmness equally so. Beyond that, good humour, common-sense and an ability to relate to, and listen to, children is important.'

Evans and Wilson (1980: 67) studied teachers' views of the characteristics of the special school most likely to cope well with children with behaviour disorders. The most important of these were:

- Warm, caring attitudes in adult–child relationships
- Improvement of self-image through success
- Individual counselling and discussion
- A varied and stimulating educational programme
- Continuity of adult–child relationships
- Firm, consistent discipline.

A number of suggestions for dealing with children with behaviour problems were given in Chapter 7.

Children with exceptional ability

A child's ability will be revealed only if there is opportunity for it to be shown. A future virtuoso violinist needs the opportunity to learn to play the violin if his or her talent is to be developed. The same is true about abilities of all kinds. This is an important reason why the curriculum should be broad and provide many opportunities for children to discover abilities. It is also true that a teacher's enthusiasm has been an important factor in the development of many able people. Freeman (1998: 1) suggests that 'Whatever the potential, it can only develop into exceptionally high achievement in circumstances which are rich in the appropriate material and psychological learning opportunities.' She also suggests that teachers should 'Watch out for motivation and interests as clues to potential' (p. 11).

Hoyle and Wilks (1974: 26) report the findings of a study group of teachers which suggest that the primary needs of gifted children are as follows:

- Contact with their average peers.
- Contact with children of comparable ability.
- To be stretched and challenged even to the point of failure and humbling experiences.
- To be guided rather than directed through a more academic approach to a greater depth of treatment.
- To avoid being set apart but to have the opportunity to set self apart on occasions.
- To pass rapidly through elementary stages and use advanced resources.
- To pursue their own line of research.
- To be exposed to some form of counselling – and their parents too.
- To be treated like other children.
- Contact with teachers gifted in similar fields.

Dean (1996: 125–6) suggests that provision for exceptionally able children needs to be of three kinds:

- opportunity to cover the normal curriculum more quickly than other children;
- enrichment of the curriculum, i.e. the provision of work of greater depth and variety;
- extension of the curriculum, i.e. the opportunity to go further than others in relation to the same content.

Freeman (1998: 44) states 'Educational enrichment is the deliberate rounding out of the basic curriculum subjects with ideas and knowledge that enable a pupil to be aware of the wider context of a subject area.' She gives three aims for enrichment activities:

- increasing ability to analyse and solve problems;
- developing profound, worthwhile interests;
- stimulating originality, initiative and self-direction.

Children who are exceptionally able need to learn to work independently as early as possible because they are likely to finish work given to the class in a shorter time than other children and you may not be able to spend as much time with them as you would like suggesting the next step. They need to develop study skills such as the following over time in the primary school. They need to be able to:

- plan a project or an enquiry;
- make judgements and hypotheses about what is planned;
- collect information from a variety of sources including first-hand; observation, discussion with other people, the Internet and books;
- take notes from observation, discussion, interviews, the Internet and books;
- evaluate the material which has been collected in the light of the original plan or hypothesis;
- select and organise the material which has been collected for presentation in a variety of forms;
- make presentations in forms such as speech, writing, audio- or video-tape, matching the report to the audience;
- evaluate the presentation.

Very able children need to develop skill in assessing their own work. You can help this development by the questions you ask about a finished piece of work.

The advantages of collaborative group work were discussed in detail in Chapter 8. It is particularly valuable for able children who may gain both from being part of a group of able children and also from working with a mixed ability group where they have to explain their ideas to others.

Maltby (1984: 209) sums up the message for teachers dealing with exceptionally able children: 'Gifted children are individuals and therefore provision for each child should be considered according to the individual personality of the child and teacher concerned. There is no correct way to provide for gifted children, only a way for each child.'

12

WORKING WITH PARENTS

Jones (1993: 44) notes that parents, by law, can:

- express a preference of school for their children where this is practicable;
- participate in the management of their children's school as elected parent governors;
- attend an annual governors' meeting for parents and pass resolutions;
- receive information about the school prescribed by statutory regulations, including the outcomes of the assessment of existing pupils;
- receive an annual report on the progress made by their children, including plans of their work within the National Curriculum;
- discuss this report with a named teacher at the school;
- be consulted by governors on the provision of sex education at school;
- be involved, where appropriate, in the assessment and review of children with special needs;
- in 1993, under new national arrangements for inspection, receive a summary of the inspection report and governors' plans to tackle any problem areas;
- have an opportunity to contribute their views to the inspection team.

These are things which the school *must* do to liaise with parents. Schools and teachers need to go beyond this stage and have a closer relationship with parents than this list implies if children are really going to benefit. There are many advantages for you as the teacher in working closely with parents. Parents know their children much more fully than you can ever do and you need to be ready to draw on this knowledge. Atkin *et al.* (1988: 7) suggest that when parents:

- understand what the school is trying to do
- identify with its main goals and support its efforts
- understand something of their role as educators
- take an active interest in, and provide support for their children's school work

then the effects can be dramatic and long-lasting.

Macbeth (1994: 303) gives five reasons why parents are relevant to what happens inside school:

1   Parents are responsible in law for their child's education, and in that sense they may be regarded as the school's legal clients.
2   If most of a child's education happens outside school, especially in the home, and if parents are co-educators of the child with teachers, then it seems logical to make the two elements of school learning and home learning compatible, and for teachers to use that home learning as a resource.
3   Research indicates that family-based learning influences the effectiveness of school on a child. It may be a significant factor among the complexity of forces associated with inequality of educational opportunity.
4   Besides providing a professional service for parents, the teacher is also an agent of the education authority and the State to some degree. There are implied functions of checking upon parents' fulfilment of duties (e.g. with regard to school attendance), and, arguably, of being an educational safety-net for pupils with incompetent or uncaring parents.
5   It seems democratically reasonable, in a decentralised system in which important decisions are made at school and class levels, that those with a stake in the school should influence (though not necessarily determine) the nature of those decisions. Parents are stakeholders on behalf of their child and should be able to influence the school policy through representatives.

Parents represent a considerable resource in many ways. There is strong evidence that where parents read with their children at home, the children make better progress in reading. Parental support for children is important for their achievement in school. Parental attitudes to school influence children's attitudes to school and to learning. Many parents also have knowledge and skills which may not only benefit their own children but could be shared more widely if the parent concerned is willing. Many teachers benefit from parental help in the classroom.

In schools where parent/teacher liaison is taken seriously the following are likely to occur:

- Parents are made welcome when they visit the school.
- Teachers listen to parents and benefit from their knowledge of their own children.
- Parents are regarded as partners in the education of children; they are consulted on many aspects of the life and work of the school and their views are taken seriously.
- Parents are kept informed about what children are learning and how parents can help with the work in hand.
- The school makes use of the skills and knowledge of parents for the benefit of children.
- Effort is made to contact parents who do not come to the school and parents who are not English-speaking.

The last twenty years or so have seen considerable changes in family life. Divorce rates have increased and Britain now has the highest rate of divorce of any European country. The proportion of single parent families has increased and around 14 per cent of all dependent children now live in one-parent families. Unemployment has also had an effect on family life and many mothers are working outside the home. These changes have had considerable implications for schools. Teachers may have to cope with children going through traumatic experiences at home. Boys may be growing up without a male model in the home which makes it more important for primary schools to have some male teachers. Some children may be going home to an empty house. Single parents may also find it more difficult to come to meetings at school, especially if they have younger children at home. Teachers need to be careful not to assume that parents who don't come to school are uninterested in their children's progress.

Tizard *et al.* (1988: 176), studying young children in inner city schools, found that while only a third of teachers felt that parents would provide the back-up at home that they would like, 'the great majority of parents told us that they wanted to help with their child's education – only 20 per cent said that it was a matter to be left to the teachers'. 'In the first two years of school, 40 per cent of parents said they heard their child read five times a week.' They found that 'the level of help given at home was much higher than had been anticipated by the reception teachers'. They also found that 'black parents gave their children significantly more help with school work than did the white parents' (p. 94).

Finding out what children are learning

Parents want to know what their children are doing at school and how they are getting on. They use all the clues they can find to puzzle things out. When they visit the school they observe the general ethos and look at children's work on display. They ask their children questions about what they are doing and get them to show their work. Of course they learn from discussion with teachers but some of the evidence suggests that this does not necessarily meet parents' needs. Tizard *et al.* (1988: 91) found that parents were not given much information about how their child was doing relative to other children. They found that 'teachers were more likely to have told parents that their child was doing well than that she was not'. Only 20 per cent of parents had been given indication that their child was having difficulties although testing suggested that a much larger proportion were not doing well. Similarly with behaviour problems. Only 12 per cent of parents had been told of these at reception level, whereas teachers reckoned that there were 26 per cent with such problems. A survey of parents in Surrey before the Education Reform Act found that parents most wanted to know where their children stood in relation to other children. This problem may have been alleviated by the requirement to report children's performance in the SATs to parents.

Hughes *et al.* (1994) studied some of the things that parents wanted from the primary school over a period of three years. They found that over half the parents in the third year of the study would have liked to know more about what their children were learning in English, mathematics and science. They would have liked a short information sheet saying what would be covered in the next few weeks. They found that: 'Virtually all parents (98 per cent) said they wanted to know more about assessment. . . . They wanted to know why assessment was being undertaken, how it would be carried out, what it would involve for their children and what their role as parents would be' (p. 157).

Homework

Many primary schools now expect children to do some form of homework and those that have the most successful practice work closely with parents. At the early stages of education parents are asked to work with their children perhaps reading to them or hearing them read, helping them to learn number bonds and later tables, to learn spellings or play games which reinforce learning. At the later stages of primary education rather more is demanded of the children but parental support is still important. Children need a quiet place to work and encouragement to get down to their homework. They may need help with using resources such as books, computers and encyclopedias where these are available at home or encouragement to use the resources of the public library. Parents may help their children where homework involves exploring a topic in the environment.

Schools which are most successful in their homework programme take care to keep parents informed about the homework which will be expected and the time it is due for completion. Homework policies are shared with parents and there is often a homework diary which parents are asked to sign when work is completed and where appropriate to comment on how the child has managed. Some schools have a form of home/school diary through which teacher and parent can correspond about the child's work. This may be particularly valuable for children with special needs.

Parents' views of schools and teachers

Much criticism has been levelled at schools in recent years and it is satisfying to know that whenever parents have been asked about their satisfaction with their children's school the answers have generally been positive. For example, Hughes *et al.* (1994) studied parents' reactions to their children's school over three years, coding their responses into 'very happy, happy, happy with reservations, mixed feelings and not happy'. In the first year 87 per cent were very happy, happy or happy with reservations and only 14 per cent were unhappy or had mixed feelings. In the second year the figures were 79 per cent and 14 per cent and in the third year 89 per cent and 10 per cent.

Pollard and Bourne (1994) surveyed parents' views of what characterised a good school. They found that relationships between parents, teachers and children came top of the list, chosen by 72 parents. This was followed by staff (63 parents), the atmosphere (53 parents) the ethos of the school (52 parents), good discipline (38 parents). Academic results came low with only 16 parents listing it.

Hughes *et al.* (1994: 122) describe parents' views of a good teacher:

> They . . . considered a good teacher to be one who was lively, enthusiastic and stimulating, who built up a good relationship with children and parents and who maintained control in the classroom and playground. Furthermore, the great majority of parents felt that these criteria were being met by their children's schools and teachers.

Communication with parents

Communication with parents is very important. Schools in a number of countries build a relationship with the class teacher in a primary school through class meetings where the teacher is able to tell parents about what he or she is planning for the children for the next term or so and suggest ways in which they can help. This is a good way to keep parents informed and provides an opportunity for parents to meet in a smaller group and give feedback on how their children appear to be coping with the work in hand.

Class newsletters are another possibility. These too could give information about current and future work and invite parental cooperation. As with all home/school communications it will be important to avoid jargon and keep the language clear. In schools with a number of children whose home language is not English, it may be necessary to invite a parent to translate the newsletter for parents who do not read English.

School reports

An important piece of communication with parents is the report on the child's achievements and progress. Ideally this should be sent home at a time when it can be followed by a meeting with parents to discuss its content. Macbeth (1989: 34, 35) suggests that written school reports have the following purposes:

1   To enable teachers to render account for their service to parents.
2   To enable teachers and parents to exchange periodic information, views and predictions about the development of a child, both academically and pastorally.
3   To assist and focus the assessment procedure.
4   To assist pupils to understand and assess themselves, to increase their self-sufficiency and to change their performance.
5   To provide an agenda for any of:
     a)   parent–pupil discussions,
     b)   teacher–pupil discussions,
     c)   parent–teacher discussions,
     d)   parent–teacher–pupil discussions.
6   To provide a basis for communication between the school and other parts of the education service about a pupil.
7   To furnish both school and family with a record of progress.

Hughes *et al.* (1994) found that three-quarters of the parents in their study wanted information in the report about the child's progress in each subject. Over a third wanted information about weaknesses so that they could help at home. They also wanted information about the child's behaviour, social skills and attitude to work.

Activities involving parents

Much work has been done in recent years to involve parents in helping their children at home, particularly with reading. A number of ways of doing this were suggested in the chapter on literacy and also in that on mathematics. Parents can be involved in many other aspects of work in the classroom. Topic work generally can be pursued at home as well as at school, especially if you give some written information for parents about what is involved. Bastiani (1989: 89) suggests the following home tasks which might be given to pupils which could involve help from parents:

- Language-based games and activities.
- Environmental topics and activities.
- The science of everyday life.
- Making things, collecting things, describing things, classifying things.
- Undertaking various kinds of research, involving family and neighbourhood history etc.

Parent/teacher meetings

All schools now arrange opportunities for parents to meet their child's class teacher to discuss his or her progress. This is an important meeting for both parents and teacher and there is a certain amount of evidence that such meetings are not always as successful as both parties would wish. Bastiani (1989: 67) found that 'while both teachers and parents continue to support strongly the *idea* of the usefulness of such contacts, there is clear evidence that both find the actual *experience* of such events disappointing, unproductive, and often deeply frustrating'. He suggests that teachers should try tape-recording such sessions and listening to them afterwards. He also suggests questionnaire surveys of how parents regarded their meeting with teachers.

He goes on to note that:

> Some teachers undoubtedly view the event with trepidation; those who are young and childless may fear the older and more experienced parent; others are afraid their professional knowledge will be challenged with questions they cannot answer; some may be concerned that their teaching methods will not meet with approval, while others may be apprehensive that they may be blamed for the child's failure to make progress.
>
> (Bastiani 1989: 73)

Teachers for their part may be hesitant about telling parents about the problems their children are experiencing. Parents and teachers may have different agendas for the meeting. Some parents will be assessing the teacher and his or her attitudes. Some will want very specific information about their child's performance and want to know how they can best help their child. There will also be parents who have unhappy memories of their own schooling and are afraid of appearing ignorant; others who are hesitant to say what they really think because they are afraid this may rebound on their child. If the child is not making good progress parents may feel it is the teacher's fault and become aggressive and defensive and doubtful about the teacher's skill and teaching methods.

There is much to be said for stating the issues you would like to discuss with parents in the letter of invitation and giving parents the chance to identify their concerns in writing before the meeting so that you can come prepared for whatever they may ask.

It is also important to make good preparation for meeting parents. Make sure you have all the information about each child well documented, with the children's work books available for parents to look at. Go over in your mind the things that you will want to say about each child, particularly where a child has not been making good progress or is posing behaviour problems. In these cases think out the positive things you can say and say these first but be definite about the problems and go on to consider how parents could help. It is important that you don't give false impressions to parents. Think out questions you might ask of the parents. You not only need to listen to them but to be seen to be listening.

You may have to deal with parents who are anxious and some who are hostile. Rowlands and Birkett (1992: 96) suggest that when you are dealing with people who are concerned or agitated you should:

- listen attentively and show that you are doing so;
- listen open-mindedly; this concern comes through to the other party;
- keep control of your features, smile when you can;
- show that you appreciate the importance of the issue;
- use the other person's name quite often;
- be courteous and friendly;
- let the other person see you expect normal behaviour.

No one finds it easy to accept criticism. It can be difficult to listen carefully when you feel that someone is being unjust and negative, but it is important that you are clear about what is being said so that you can deal with it. Take a deep breath before responding and be ready to react honestly, accepting criticism where the other person seems to have a valid point. It can be disarming when someone says 'Yes, I agree with the point you are making and am trying to do something about it.' Try to avoid becoming defensive and show that you are taking the criticism seriously. Explain where this seems necessary and acknowledge the other person's feelings. If at all possible, try to agree a course of action including arrangements for reporting back to each other on how the work is progressing.

Stacey (1991: 98) makes the following points about talking with parents:

- Be honest and specific.
- Be flexible. Seek the parents' opinion so that you can work together on solutions and ideas.
- Observe carefully. Notice how you are feeling and how that is affecting the discussion. Recognise that parents may be feeling

146

inhibited or tense and give time for them to take in what you are saying and offer their views.

- Listen. Concentrate and show you are listening by adopting an appropriate posture and by seeking clarification, reflecting and summarising.

- Help the parents relax. They are on your territory. Give them a chance to contribute to the conversation.

- Allow silences for thought and reflection. Many of us have been brought up to believe that silences are awkward. Yet talking can be an interruption and disruptive. Silences allow people time to collect their thoughts and continue.

- Be positive about the child. Give examples, not generalities.

- Ask questions which lead the conversation on. Avoid putting answers in the parent's mouth. Allow questions which are difficult or challenging for you.

- Answer questions honestly. Avoid justifying or going on the defence. If it is difficult for you to say, express the feeling. If you do not know the answer, admit this. Do not make promises which you know you cannot fulfil or reassure with improbabilities.

- Remember, good relationships take time. Allow the relationship to grow. It is not friendship but a viable working partnership that you are seeking. This means that you do not have to agree on everything but it means you need to respect and value each other's experience.

It is a good idea, if you can find the time, to make brief notes of your conversations with parents so that you can refer back to them next time you meet. The parents will remember what you said to them much more easily than you will because they have only one interview to remember, while you have many. A brief note will help you to be more ready for the next meeting.

A survey of parents undertaken some time ago in Surrey primary schools revealed that parents felt strongly about privacy for their talks with class teachers. They were not happy with interviews which were held in the hall or in the classroom with other parents waiting within earshot.

Parents who don't come to the school are a concern for most teachers. They may have difficulty in leaving their children to come to events in the evening and may be working outside the home during the day. Fathers, in particular, may find it difficult to get to the school except in the evening. Try to get to know the family so that you understand any difficulties the parents may have in visiting the school. When possible, personalise communication by addressing the parents by name. With older children it is possible to get each child to write in the name of his or her parents or carers on a duplicated letter. There is also much to be said for making a home visit. Teachers who have experienced home visiting generally find that they are made very welcome and that the effort they have made to visit is much appreciated. They also find that such visits are very revealing about the children they teach and enable them to understand more fully the way the child behaves in school.

Parent surveys

Another way of finding out what parents think is to make a questionnaire survey. This can easily be done for one class at a time and can include questions such as the following:

- Do you feel that you are getting sufficient information about the work your child is doing in school? Is there any other information you would like?
- We welcome parents helping their children with school work at home. Is there any help you would like with this?
- Is the amount and type of homework your child is receiving posing any particular problems?
- Would you like more opportunities to see the school/class in action?
- Have you any particular skills or interests which you would be willing to share with the children or staff?

The questionnaire could also include questions about particular pieces of work in which you have tried to involve parents as well as children.

Parents helping in the classroom

Many schools now involve parents as classroom helpers or in tasks which would otherwise have to be done by the teacher. Mortimore *et al.* (1988) found that this had a beneficial effect on children's progress. They also found that teachers' fears that parents might want to take over in the classroom were unfounded. 'The experience of those who have worked with parents in classrooms is that the most usual problem is the reluctance of parents to play as full a part as the teacher would like, rather than the parent taking over.' Bastiani (1989: 84) lists the following ways in which parents can provide more individual attention for children:

- Hearing children read (including the more fluent readers who can be overlooked).
- Using flashcards.
- Help with spelling and writing.
- Extra opportunities for discussion with adults.

- Coaching individuals in sporting activities.
- Special help with disruptive child.
- Help with computer work.

We might add to this list playing literacy and numeracy games with children and helping to supervise on school trips. Schools where there are considerable numbers of ethnic minority children may like to involve their parents in helping to translate information for other parents, telling stories in their home language to groups of children and then, if possible, discussing them in English. They may also talk to other children about festivals and customs in their home country.

Parents may also help by typing out stories at a child's dictation which can then be used as reading material for that child. They may be helpful to children using the library, helping them to find the information they need. They can also prepare materials and displays of work.

It is important in involving parents in this way to brief them adequately. It is very easy to assume that a parent will know what to do and that she will react as you would to a given situation. It is important that you are both telling the same tale. Parents may need to be told what to do when a child asks for a spelling, or when they hear a child read and he or she has difficulty with a particular word. If parents are helping with a school trip they need briefing on what you are hoping children will get from the experience and how the parents can best contribute.

Parents may also be nervous about helping in the classroom and you need to help them to relax and find out how they can contribute. You too may be nervous about having another adult in the classroom and this may rub off on the children and the parent who is helping. These are problems which gradually disappear as you get to know each other. Stacey (1991: 47) comments 'Those teachers who start to work directly with parents in the education of the children find that it leads to more understanding and therefore more support from parents for the learning processes which go on in school.'

Home/school agreements

Schools have to have home/school agreements in place from September 1999. Berkshire Education Authority (Berkshire County Council 1993: 3) suggests that the main aim of having a home/school compact or agreement is 'to improve standards by helping each pupil to achieve his or her best in all aspects of school life'. They give the general purposes of a compact as follows:

- to personalise and make more explicit what a school offers its pupils and what parents and the community can offer;

149

- to develop agreed common expectations and goals, and to eliminate distrust;
- to provide mutual support for young people as they grow up;
- to make the best possible use of all the resources available to the school;
- to improve exchange of information between teachers, parents and pupils;
- to heighten awareness of what each partner expects of the others, and to provide a starting point for discussion if one of the partners appears not to be playing their part.

Such agreements should help parents to feel that they have an important part to play in their children's education and complement the work of the school by supporting their child's learning. Teachers should be in a better position to work with parents and pupils should experience a greater consistency of demand between home and school.

The DfEE paper of guidance on home/school agreements (1998c: 15) states that 'agreements will be best when they are:

- a product of a genuine discussion between all parties concerned; including the pupil;
- balanced, fair and even-handed;
- agreed and not imposed;
- introduced as part of a whole-school approach to working with parents;
- clear and meaningful to parents. It is important to get the tone and style right, so that all parties are clear about what is expected of them;
- translated where the parent does not read English; or communicated orally where the parent has difficulty with reading;
- workable, not over-detailed and allowing for different family background and circumstance;
- reviewed regularly.

Skills needed for working with parents

McConkey (1985: 84) suggests that teachers need the following core skills for working with parents:

- flexibility to cope with a diversity of people and needs.
- a willingness to listen, observe and negotiate.
- a respect for parents' viewpoints that is shown by you consulting them at least as often as they consult you.

- being open about your feelings so that parents can be open about theirs.
- a willingness to answer parents' questions and listening to the answers they give to your questions.
- sharing responsibility for decision making with parents.

Teacher training rarely includes training in working with parents, and the school in which you find yourself has a strong influence on the way parents approach the school and the way in which teachers are expected to respond. Your relationship with parents has a considerable influence on the way the parents in their turn support their children's learning. It is worth putting considerable effort into working with them.

Jones (1993: 49) suggests that

a true partnership between home and school can bring about:

- positive attitudes
- positive self-image
- improved performance
- improved effort
- improved motivation
- support for teaching
- informed help from parents
- better parental understanding
- a shared purpose and belonging.

13

EVALUATION AND RECORD KEEPING

assessments come in many forms o can be carried out in various ways eg?

As a teacher you will be assessing children's learning all the time as you work with your class. As you talk to the class or lead discussion you observe, almost without thinking about it, the way that children are responding to you. Children's answers to your questions and the ideas they suggest give you clues to the way they are thinking. You learn more as you ask further questions and probe to discover the extent of their understanding. Drummond (1993: 129) sums this up by saying 'The educator's observations and assessments are the means by which educational provision becomes more effective, more closely attuned to individuals, and richer in opportunities for all.' She also points out that 'Assessment practices are based on the personal value systems of the teachers who make the assessments' (p. 126).

The Task Group on Assessment and Testing (DES 1987: para 23) suggests that

> information derived from assessments (including tests) shall be capable of serving several purposes:
>
> - *formative*, so that the positive achievements of a pupil may be recognised and discussed and the appropriate next steps may be planned;
> - *diagnostic*, through which learning difficulties may be scrutinised and classified so that appropriate remedial help and guidance can be provided;
> - *summative*, for the recording of overall achievement of a pupil in a systematic way;
> - *evaluative*, by means of which some aspects of the work of a school, an LEA or other discrete part of the educational service can be assessed and/or reported upon.

The legal requirement for assessment in schools has brought about a renewed concern with evaluation on the part of teachers. Gipps *et al*. (1995) studied the effect of the requirement to assess children as part of testing at Key

Stages 1 and 2. They found that many teachers had begun to collect evidence of children's work as proof of progress and achievement. This included such things as tape-recordings of reading and photographs as well as written work. They also made greater use of observation to assess children, especially in mathematics and science. They also kept more complete records, questioning children closely to determine understanding, and planned assessment into their teaching.

Evaluation is the final stage in the process of monitoring and assessing children's work, progress and behaviour. You observe and monitor and assess and then reflect on your findings in order to decide what to do next. Pollard and Bourne (1994: 220) suggest the following principles of assessment:

- Assessment must be used as a continuous part of the teaching-learning process, involving pupils, wherever possible, as well as teachers in identifying next steps.
- Assessment for any purpose should serve the purpose of improving learning by exerting a positive force on the curriculum at all levels.
- Assessment must provide an effective means of communication with parents and other partners in the learning enterprise in a way which helps them support pupils' learning.
- The choice of different assessment procedures must be decided on the basis of the purpose for which the assessment is being undertaken. This may well mean employing different techniques for different assessment purposes.
- Assessment must be used fairly as part of information for judging the effectiveness of schools. This means taking into account contextual factors which, as well as the quality of teaching, affect the achievement of pupils.
- Citizens have a right to detailed and reliable information about the standards being achieved across the nation through the educational system.

It is important that assessment is valid whether it is simply to inform you as teacher or to inform parents or to help a child to see his or her own progress. This means that you need to check one piece of evidence against another to see if they agree. Gipps *et al.* (1995: 26) record the comment of one teacher as follows: 'A lot of assessment used to be gut feeling but now I am going back and checking. I'm observing children far more thoroughly and doing more talking to them.'

It is also important to consider process as well as product. Was the way you introduced a topic the best possible? How effective was your questioning? Did you range across the class sufficiently in selecting children to respond? Are children developing understanding as well as knowledge and skills? Are they becoming independent learners, able to make sensible decisions about how to act about learning something? Are they becoming thinkers?

In assesing children's work and behaviour you need to remember that many of the judgements you make are subjective. Each teacher has a personal set of values and ideas about what constitutes achievement and progress for a given child and these will vary from one teacher to another. It is therefore valuable to discuss children's work with colleagues so that you can check on your judgements. This is another way of ensuring that your assessments are valid.

Areas for evaluation

As teacher, you need to evaluate the achievement, progress and behaviour of pupils and you own teaching performance. Assessing achievement and progress includes assessing the stage of development a child has reached and discovering the approaches and strategies individual children use in their work, particularly when they appear to be having difficulties. You also need to assess the extent that children are becoming independent learners, able to assess work for themselves and developing the skills needed for further learning.

Assessing social development and learning

Behaviour assessment not only involves assessing whether children conform to the rules obtaining in the classroom and school, but also their ability to relate to adults and other children, share with others, take part in discussion, contribute to group work both as leaders and followers, listen and respond to each other, see from another's point of view and adjust ideas in the light of reflection and discussion. You need to consider the degree of self-confidence children appear to have and their ability to be independent in their work and general behaviour. Are they developing social skills?

Assessing performance of different groups of children

There are also broad areas to consider. How does the progress and achievement of boys and girls compare? Are children from ethnic minorities doing less well than other children? Is there a marked difference related to the social background of different children? Are any particular approaches more or less successful with any of these groups? Ofsted (1996: 41) notes that schools need to consider 'the monitoring of performance of specific groups of pupils within their schools and the implications of findings for subsequent action; for example, the under-achievement of boys'.

Assessing your own performance

As the teacher you need to evaluate your own performance lesson by lesson, day by day and long term. Kyriacou (1991: 126) suggests the following questions as an agenda for reflection and evaluation following a particular lesson:

1   Did this lesson go well?
   ● Were the learning activities envisaged successfully implemented?
   ● What did the pupils learn in the lesson?
   ● How can I be sure such learning occurred?
   ● Did the lesson and learning reflect my intended aims?
2   Did any pupil or group of pupils fail to benefit (e.g. able pupils, average pupils, less able pupils, shy pupils, male pupils, female pupils, a pupil who missed previous lessons, disruptive pupils)? If so, could this have been avoided?
3   What changes can I usefully make before giving a similar lesson to another class?
4   What have I learnt about this class, or particular pupils, that might influence future lessons with this class?
5   What have I learnt about this topic or subject matter that might influence future lessons?
6   Are there any immediate actions I should take following this lesson (e.g. did any pupil appear to indicate some special educational need)?
7   Am I satisfied with my general planning of this lesson, and its presentation and monitoring? Did this lesson sustain pupils' attention and interest, and did it appear to be intellectually and pedagogically sound?
8   Did any problems occur in the lesson that I should take note of?
9   How can I consolidate the learning which occurred and relate it to future demands and applications?

It is a good idea to work with a colleague evaluating each other's work if time can be found for this, looking at what is happening and how children are reacting, and looking for what is succeeding and what is less successful. Discussing children's work with a colleague is also very useful and is a way of validating your views and guarding against inbuilt prejudices. It is particularly helpful when this can be done across year groups. It is also useful to compare notes about children with the teacher who had them the previous year.

Forms of evaluation

Observation

Observation is fundamental to evaluation. As teacher you are observing all the time. You make hundreds of observations and adjustments every day. You note automatically how children react to what you present to them and adjust to their reaction. You check on the way children are working or not working. You notice children who are day-dreaming or about to become disruptive. You use your inbuilt knowledge of body language to make judgements about how children are behaving and whether they are with you or not.

Much of this evaluation is automatic. What is needed also is conscious observation and judgement making. The demands of the National Curriculum and associated assessments have made teachers everywhere much more conscious of the need to observe and make judgements intentionally. Chazan *et al.* (1987: 12) make the point that:

> To provide the most fruitful experiences and to encourage children to explore and discover for themselves can only be successfully accomplished on the basis of careful observation of the children concerned over a period of time. Teachers must therefore be observers in order to provide the structured framework for learning.

They also note the importance of systematic observation and monitoring. You need a system for working round the children in your class so that you observe each of them carefully over a period of time, looking at particular aspects of their work. This may be linked to individual interviews about work or hearing children read and discussing what they have read. Thus you might aim to observe and talk with one or two children each day, perhaps investigating their understanding of an aspect of number work or looking at how they are progressing in a particular topic.

It is important to remember that a child may know more than he or she is able to demonstrate on a given occasion. Vygotsky's theory of a 'zone of proximal development' suggests that a child can go beyond the knowledge he or she appears to have with 'scaffolding' from another person, usually a teacher.

Observation has the advantage that it can take in more than a test situation. In hearing a child read, for example, you may not only be checking on how well the child recognised the words in the text, but also his or her understanding of what is being read and the mistakes being made and their possible significance.

One disadvantage of observation for assessment is that you only see what your experience, background and frame of reference allow. You may miss

156

things because you have not experienced them before or because you are not looking out for them. This is why it is important to study children and their work with colleagues from time to time so that you enlarge your vision of what there is to see. This is particularly important at the beginning of your teaching career but it is also possible for an experienced teacher to miss things because teaching has become a matter of habit.

Individual interviews

Both the literacy and numeracy programmes recommend that you spend time with children as individuals over a period investigating their thinking and helping them to set targets for their next pieces of work. Ofsted (1996: 26) suggests that there is not enough systematic monitoring. 'The need to improve the curriculum by means of systematic monitoring and evaluation of classroom practice is often recognised, but does not as yet take place sufficiently to have a major impact on quality.'

It is not easy for teachers to fit in individual interviews because of the many demands on them by the children. You need to see that the rest of the class has work which does not require too much of your attention and train children to seek other sources than the teacher for help. Try to make it a rule that when you are talking with an individual child or hearing someone read, you are not to be interrupted for spellings or enquiries about what to do next. Encourage children to ask each other, use dictionaries or word lists about the classroom. See that they always know what to do when they have finished a piece of work if you are not available. Making time to talk with individuals is largely a matter of good organisation.

Testing

All teachers need to test children from time to time to assess what they have learned and what still has to be covered. The problem with many tests including some standardised tests is that they can be more a test of reading than a test of what is known. It is helpful to try to accumulate over a period a number of tests that you can use more than once and develop them so that you can feel some confidence that they test what you are setting out to test. It is useful to look at the mistakes children make and to see if these stem from a misunderstanding of the test question. Studying children's understanding of what is asked will be particularly important with baseline testing of children entering school for the first time.

Although the Standard Assessment Tasks (SATs) now offer a means of assessing how well children are doing in English, mathematics and science at Key Stages 1 and 2, there is still a place for the use of standardised tests which may be particularly helpful in between the SATs assessments along with the optional national tests. You need to know how well your children are doing in comparison with other children of their age and standardised tests give you valuable information about this.

There is a difference between testing for mastery and testing in order to group children for learning or to see how children compare with one another. In the first case you might expect most children to score well. In the second case you need a spread of scores. A diagnostic test, whether standardised or home-made, may have scores of any kind because the object is to discover difficulties in order to remedy them.

Looking at children's work

Children's written work and their performance in oral work provides one of the most important sources of information about their understanding and their progress. It can be helpful to keep examples of work at various stages during the year. These may include tape-recorded examples of reading or contribution to discussion. There are various ways of doing this. In one school, children were given loose-leaf files into which they put any piece of work which they and the teacher agreed was good. These files were shown proudly to visitors and were taken home to show parents. In another school, children did a week's work in a special exercise book once a term and these exercise books made a good record of each child's progress over time. The teacher might also select examples for a folder of each child's work.

It is particularly useful in looking at children's work to study the mistakes they make. Mistakes in spelling can be analysed to see if they are the result of a lack of understanding of simple rules about spelling. The child who spells the word 'danced' as 'danct', for example has not grasped the rule for the way we spell words in the past tense. The child who spells 'filled' as 'filed' has not learned the rule about doubling the consonant when the vowel which precedes it is short. Similarly in mathematics an analysis of children's mistakes and discussion about them will often lead to better understanding and improvement when simply 'doing corrections' may not.

Self-assessment and peer-assessment

Children need to learn to assess their own work and progress and this can be helped by small group or paired discussions about each others' work. This activity needs to start with discussion about the criteria which might be used in making assessments. Muschamp (1996: 281) studied children's assessments of work and found that they were almost entirely concerned with the work's appearance and things like handwriting and drawings. Further questioning produced ideas like 'The answers are all right.' 'I haven't repeated words like 'and then' and I have included describing words.' 'When asked why they thought they were doing a particular activity very few children understood the specific aims of the teacher.'

The study went on to establish learning objectives with the children and the skills, knowledge and understanding that each activity was designed to foster. Children learned to look out for things like good beginnings to stories, measuring accurately to the nearest centimetre and concentrating on the sequence of an account. The children were given technical language to talk about their work and questions they could ask themselves about their work. They were encouraged to ask questions like 'What do I know now?' When the objective was to develop understanding the child was encouraged to ask 'Can I explain?' Time was set aside to discuss with children what they had learned from any particular activity.

> In some activities it was difficult for pupils to decide if any learning had taken place at all, even though teachers were confident that the activities had been of value. There were particular types of activity that fell into this category: practice, art, enjoyment and religious education'. Practice and reinforcement did not always lead to any new learning.
>
> Enjoyment experienced in many activities, for example, reading or watching a dramatic performance, seemed to make children uncertain about what they had actually learned.
>
> (Muschamp 1996: 282–3)

Needham (1994) suggests a range of ways of helping children to assess their own work. A child can be asked to read someone else's work and write a review of it. Links can be set up between two classes or even between two schools in which the children share information about their achievements and need to explain what they have done and how or why they did it. Children can write about the work that they have done saying how they feel about it. They can complete unfinished sentences such as 'Something I'm good at is . . .' or 'Something I'd like to be good at is . . . (p. 159). You can also ask questions like 'What do you think of this piece of work? What do you like about it? How could you make it better?

The important thing in helping children to assess their own work is to discuss with them some of the criteria you are using to make judgements about their work and to get them to use these in judging their own work and that of their peers. It is a good idea to start this work by asking them what they think you are using as criteria and then to build on the answers you get.

Level descriptions

As a result of National Assessment teachers have begun to use level descriptions which Pollard (1996b: 51) describes as 'what a teacher might characteristically expect a pupil to know and be able to do or understand if he or she is to be assessed as attaining that level. The required teacher judgement is of what level description is the "best fit" with the child's performance.' Most teachers by now will be fairly skilled at assessing level descriptions but there is still much to be said for discussing each child's work with someone else in order to validate your own views.

Recording

It is now a statutory requirement to keep records of the achievement and progress of individual children and to provide at least an annual report to parents. Spear (1990: 147) notes that the Statutory Instrument (DES 1989c) No. 1261 The Education (School Records) Regulations says four basic things about the governors' responsibility for record-keeping in their school:

1   A curricular record must be kept on each pupil and it must be updated annually.
2   Upon receipt of a written request the record must be made available to an 'entitled' person and copies made available, at cost, for purchase. (An entitled person is a parent or a pupil over sixteen.)
3   An entitled person may ask for the record to be amended or have his disagreement appended to the record.
4   Schools have the right to obtain the record of a newly-enrolled pupil from his previous school.

Records of achievement

Schools are now required to keep a record of achievement for each child which should be passed on to the next school when the child leaves. This involves having a folder for each child which contains the following:

1   Formal personal records.
2   National Curriculum attainment record, test scores, teacher assessment and diagnostic information.
3   Records of pupils' personal and social skills, interests, activities, achievements within and outside school.
4   Reports to parents, pupils' self-assessments and records of meetings between pupil and teacher in order to review work and targets set.
5   Examples of work and evidence of achievement.

There is much to be said for reviewing each child's record with him or her, helping to decide what should be recorded, the targets which might be set and ways in which they might be assessed. Individual target-setting is required as part of the literacy strategy and will be required for numeracy also. Out of school activities are an important part of the record and you can learn a good deal about a child by discussing what he or she does out of school hours. Membership of Cubs and Brownies and other children's organisations, ways in which the child helps at home or looks after younger siblings, work on a home computer, making things of various kinds, hobbies, music lessons, membership of dance classes and many other similar activities might be recorded. It is a good idea for the child to record this type of information for him- or herself

Many teachers are now keeping examples of children's work by way of a record of what they are achieving but there is also a need to keep other records of achievement, progress and behaviour. It is important to make these as simple to keep and as little time-consuming as possible while at the same time making them comprehensive and easy to interpret. They also need to be made with an eye on future action since the main purpose of keeping records is to inform future action.

Records are objective only when they deal with what is testable and even then subjective judgements can be made about test results. Teachers need to be aware that they are vulnerable to prejudice. It is easy to have low expectations of a child because his speech is non-standard or because you know he comes from a deprived home background and in this situation you tend to see behaviour which confirms your assumptions rather than behaviour which contradicts them. There is a good deal of evidence to suggest that children perform better when much is expected of them.

Records of children can be of various types:

Notes on children

There is much to be said for keeping a file with a page for each child on which you note any special progress or behaviour which appears in the course of the day. When you use individual interviews the results of these and the targets agreed can be noted. When a page is filled it can be placed in the child's main file and you then have a record which may be useful when writing reports or making judgements about the level a child has reached. This sort of record is particularly useful for children with special needs, where you need to note progress with the child's individual education plan. If you are dealing with a child who poses behaviour problems it is helpful to note the circumstances in which particular behaviours appear to arise and to chart any progress towards improvement.

You can also keep a separate, more general note of children's responses to the work you are presenting and parts of the lesson which went well or badly.

Check-lists

Another way of recording children's work, progress and behaviour is to use a check-list of particular behaviours or achievements as a means of recording observation and testing. This gives you a framework which can be helpful in directing your attention and is at the same time fairly quick to use. Items such as phonic knowledge or number bonds and tables lend themselves particularly well to this kind of record.

Children's own records

Children can also be encouraged to keep their own records of the work they have covered each day. It is useful to give each child a notebook for this purpose and to set aside time daily for them to fill it in. The notebooks will give you a useful oversight of how much work each child has done.

A different approach is to have a wall chart with each child's name and a list of the types of work you expect them to cover over a period of time. They can then tick off their name under the appropriate heading each time they complete a piece of work. This is probably a more useful method with younger children whereas the notebook is a good idea with the older ones.

Tape-recordings and photographs

Tape-recordings and photographs make very useful records of particular kinds of activities. Discussion and oral presentations can be taped and kept as part of a child's record or part of a group record in the case of discussion. Taping is also very useful for reflecting on your own performance checking on things like the way you question, the extent to which you give a wait time after asking questions or the expositions and explanations you give.

Photographs are particularly useful for recording the displays which result from a project and also for children's art work, although the work itself can be kept as a record. Video tape is also valuable for recording activities like drama and dance.

Marking

The way you mark children's work in itself constitutes a record whether you give actual marks or grades or simply write comments. You have a certain amount of choice in what you do in marking work. You can mark work with the child beside you or take it home to mark. Where it is possible, there is much to be said for marking work with the child beside you. This gives you the opportunity to question and find out about mistakes and provides an opportunity for teaching. It is particularly valuable in mathematics to be able to explore a child's thinking and discover why a particular mistake was made. However, this is difficult to do when the class is large and with older children, who may write a good deal, it is unlikely that you can mark all work with the child beside you.

Probably the most important thing to do in marking work away from the classroom is to make a written comment which directs the child's attention in some way, perhaps to the things which are good about the work and ways in which it could be even better, perhaps to the need to pay more attention to some aspect. You can choose to select only a limited number of errors in some cases so that the child concerned can concentrate on learning the correct versions. You can also use the opportunity to correct misunderstanding and mistakes and note points which you want to take up with the child in person. You can select particular pieces of work to read out which helps the self-esteem of the children concerned as well as providing examples of the kind of work you are looking for. Work can also be displayed.

It is useful with older children to arrange for them to mark each other's work from time to time, using given criteria which have been discussed. You can then check on a sample of work in more detail. Giving criteria for marking is useful in any case.

Reports to parents

Schools are now required to provide reports to parents at all stages in the school including the reception class. The Qualifications and Curriculum Authority (1999: 32) suggests that these should contain the following:

- Brief comments on the child's progress in each subject and activity studied as part of the school curriculum. These should highlight strengths and development needs.
- The child's general progress.
- Arrangements for parents to discuss the report with a teacher at the school.
- Total number of session (half days) since the child's last report or since the child entered the school, whichever is later, and the percentage missed through unauthorised absence.

Schools should also give comparative data about the achievements of children in the same year group, the same school and nationally. At the early stages of school, teachers may wish to report on the child's progress since the baseline assessment on entry which must be discussed with parents during the term in which the assessment has taken place. You may also wish to report on the results of the optional tests in the intermediate years.

The QCA paper also suggests that parents want to know how their child's performance compares with previous performance, the strengths and weaknesses, areas for development and improvement, how they can help and whether the child is happy, settled and behaving well. They also suggest that 'it is important not to obscure low achievement or under-achievement by the use of faint praise or by avoiding any mention of the problem' (p. 53).

Transfer reports

Children normally transfer from one school to the next at given points in their school career but some may change schools at any time if their parents have to move house. In all cases the sending school is required to provide a record for the receiving school. Such reports need to include the following:

- Personal information about the child.
- The primary record of achievement.
- National Curriculum assessment test records and teacher assessments.
- The child's most recent literacy and numeracy targets.
- A folder of work which includes written work which represents the best that the child can do.
- Information about special educational needs where this is applicable.

Planning evaluation

In planning evaluation on a broader basis you need to be specific about the criteria you are going to use to evaluate success. You need to state objectives in specific terms and give yourself a time by which you plan to achieve them. You then need to decide what information you will need to know whether you have achieved your objectives and how and when you will collect this.

It is wise to limit the evaluation you plan to what can be sensibly managed. Look for information which is already available which could be used and plan to collect evidence as you go along rather than leaving it to the end. This means that evaluabiont has to be planned before you start work rather than at the end. It may be a good idea to try to identify performance indicators at an early stage.

The outcomes of assessment and evaluation

Evaluation itself needs to be assessed to see if it is leading to the outcomes desired without too much stress for teacher or children. How much time and effort is it taking and is the time and effort spent worthwhile in terms of the outcomes for action?

It is also important to consider the effects of assessment and evaluation on the children. Drummond (1993: 135) makes the point that 'If assessment is to work for pupils, in terms of practical outcomes (and not just good intentions) we must not ignore the part that pupils' feelings play in the process.' The problem for the teacher is that children who do not achieve well may lose motivation and it is therefore important to recognise and praise effort. Drummond comments 'When we examine the practical outcomes of our assessment practices we must note increased or decreased motivation, enhanced or shattered self-esteem, positive or negative attitudes towards learning, an enlarged or diminished desire for understanding.'

14

THE TEACHER AS
RESEARCHER

In this book so far, we have been concerned with what researchers have had to say about classroom practice. Teachers can also be researchers. It is all part of being a self-monitoring, reflective practitioner. It helps if you can do this as part of a university-led course, because of the expertise which will be available, but it is perfectly possible to set up small research projects on your own as part of your teaching.

Classroom research is easier if teachers can work together to study what is happening in their classrooms. This is not easy in the primary school since most teachers work full time with their classes and there is not enough opportunity for teachers to spend time observing each other. However, efforts are being made in many primary schools to give curriculum coordinators time to observe and support other teachers, and classroom observation is an essential part of the appraisal process. These activities also give those concerned an opportunity to research aspects of the work in classrooms.

It is, in any case, still possible for an individual teacher to set up experiments in teaching and learning and assess their effects. Even if it is not possible to involve other teachers as observers, it is still possible to get feedback from children. Where both teacher observers and feedback from children can be provided the results will have greater validity.

There are risks of a kind in carrying out such research. The teacher who lets colleagues and children comment on his or her work risks a loss of self-esteem and you have to be ready for this in setting up a research project. Elliott (1991) found that where teachers had access to other teachers' classroom problems and to feedback from pupils, their ability to tolerate losses in self- esteem was greater. They also became better at self-monitoring their classroom practice.

Hopkins (1993: 63) suggests the following as general starting points for a group of teachers setting out to study their practice:

- I would like to improve the . . .
- Some people are unhappy about . . .
- What can I do to change the situation?

- I am perplexed by . . .
- . . . is a source of irritation. What can I do about it?
- I have an idea I would like to try out in my class.
- How can the experience of . . . be applied to . . . ?
- Just what do I do with respect to . . . ?

He suggests that teachers jot down ideas which arise from such questions and then evaluate the usefulness, viability and importance of each topic. He offers the following advice (1993: 64):

1 Do not tackle anything that you cannot do anything about.
2 Only take on, at least initially, small-scale and relatively limited topics.
3 Choose a topic that is important to you or your students, or one that you have to be involved in anyway in the course of your normal school activities.
4 As far as possible try and work collaboratively on the focus of your classroom research.
5 Make connections between your classroom research work and the school's development plan priorities or the school aims.

You might, for example, set out to study the way you use questioning, looking at such issues as the variety of questions you ask, how many involve thinking or giving explanations or opinions on the part of the children, how long you wait for responses before you call on someone to answer, the range of children who actually answer the questions, the actual learning which has taken place as a result of the session. An observer could record these things for you but you can provide information for yourself by tape-recording a session and listening carefully to the tape afterwards, checking on wait time, the range of questions asked, the quality of the responses and the way you responded to the children's answers. You may also be able to check on the range of children answering the questions if you have named them in each case. With an older class you could get two or three children to write down the initials of the children who answer questions. You might also test for the learning taking place as a result of the session.

It may be worth asking children for their feelings about questioning sessions. John Holt (1984) describes how he discussed questioning with a group of children in a class with which he felt he had good relationships. He asked how they felt when they were asked a question and got the reply 'We gulp.' Galton (1989: 73) also describes children's views about answering questions in class:

Older pupils described the strategy where they put their hands up to answer a question and put them down again if there was a likelihood of the teacher picking on them to answer. One pupil, referring to answering a question, said, 'It's like walking a tightrope'.

You can also discuss with children how they view the different activities which go on in the classroom and which they feel are the best ways of learning for them. With older children pupil diaries of what has happened can be useful if you take them into your confidence about what you are studying. You can also keep field notes, noting down what has happened that seems relevant when you get a few minutes to do this and these can be compared with pupil diaries.

Using an observer

If you are able to work with a colleague as observer it is important to define the focus of the observation together in advance. Hopkins (1993: 78) suggests that 'The more specific and more negotiated the focus of the classroom observation, the more likely it is that the "data" so gathered will be useful for developmental purposes.' He goes on to suggest that the observer needs to guard against the natural tendency to make judgements too quickly, to create an atmosphere of trust and know how to gather appropriate information on such things as movement in the classroom or types of instruction and response. An observer may observe in an open-minded way noting anything which seems significant or alternatively he or she could record only events which fit into certain categories, for example presentation, indirect teaching, direct teaching, voice, questioning strategies, feedback to children, expression of expectations and so on. A more focused observation needs to have appropriate check-lists or *aides-mémoire* and the observer needs to make good records of what is being observed. Feedback needs to be done soon after the observation while it is still fresh in the minds of both teacher and observer.

Interviews

You can learn a good deal by interviewing children about their experience of a particular piece of teaching and learning or how they view a particular aspect of classroom life. It is a good idea to talk to a small group of children rather than individuals as they often reinforce each other and spark each other off. Try to convey the idea that you value their opinions and keep your comments neutral, not showing surprise or disapproval about what they say. It is a good idea to plan out the questions you mean to ask beforehand and have a note of them beside you. Ask questions like 'What did you like best about what we did?' 'What did you like least?' 'Can you think of a better way to do this?'

Questionnaires

You can develop the interview idea further by using a questionnaire with the children. You can include similar questions to the above, but it may be easier, particularly with younger children, to give alternative answers for them to tick or ring. You can also use happy or sad faces as a way of getting opinions from younger children.

Using the data

The whole purpose of studying your teaching and organisation is to improve your classroom practice and reinforce successful strategies. This can lead to setting targets for improvement. Putting your information together and discussing it with a colleague should lead to improved practice. It is particularly helpful if you are able to get information from an observer and from children so that the results complement each other. This is a way of thinking about your work as a teacher so that you are all the time improving what you do. Hopkins (1993: 165) comments:

> I think that all teacher-researchers need to put their data together in such a way that:
>
> 1   The research can be replicated on another occasion.
> 2   The evidence used to generate hypotheses and consequent action is clearly documented.
> 3   Action taken as a result of the research is monitored.
> 4   The reader finds the research accessible and that it resonates with his or her own experience.

Evaluating the research

Hopkins (p. 168) also suggests that you need to ask yourself questions about the research you have done such as:

- Did I collect the information as planned? Did it provide the information I needed?
- What problems did I have? What could I have done better? Should I employ other data-gathering methods?
- Did I gather all relevant information? Should I have gathered pupils' opinions, parental views, other teachers' feelings?
- In what ways can I use the information to make more effective teacher decisions? Is further information required?

- Can the information obtained be interpreted in other ways? Are my interpretations and conclusions valid?
- Have I presented the information in a clear way? Does the information indicate future teaching actions?

15

CONCLUSIONS

The Education Reform Act (1988) and the National Curriculum may have had the intention to change the ideology of primary education from an informal and child-centred approach to a more formal one. While teachers have certainly made changes in the way they work there is little evidence that they have become less child-centred or completely abandoned former ways of working. Broadfoot (1996: 84), writing of the findings of the PACE (Primary Assessment, Curriculum and Experience) project with respect to the changes brought about by the Education Reform Act and the National Curriculum, reports the following conclusions:

> It is clarity of aims, assessment skills and subject knowledge which have figured most prominently as requirements of change. Against this, teaching skills, knowledge of and relationships with children have stayed as constants in the core of teachers' work. Thus there is little evidence as yet of any shift from a child-centred ideology of teaching. Rather a reconfirmation of the findings of PACE 1 that teachers will add new practices to their repertoire by law, but that in the short term at least, will seek to mediate the goals of these new practices to support their existing understanding of what primary teaching is and indeed their values concerning what it should be.

The PACE project studied fifty-four children in nine widely dispersed geographical areas and found 'relative continuity in pupils' classroom experience'. 'More than one in three teachers thought that children were getting a better educational experience following the introduction of the National Curriculum and fewer than one in twenty thought that children were getting a worse experience.' 'Many saw themselves as "mediating" new requirements deriving from a turbulent external environment' (p. 147).

Raven et al. (1985: 71) listed some of the wider aims of education:

> These included the ability to analyse social and economic situations, the confidence and initiative required to introduce change,

the ability to monitor the effects of one's actions and modify one's behaviour accordingly, the ability to apply facts and techniques which have been learned to new problems, the determination to go out into the world committed to making it a better place to live, the ability to listen to what others say and work out what lies behind what they say, the tendency to study the long term social consequences of one's actions, the tendency to be inquisitive and adventurous, the capacity to be confident with people and situations one has not met before, the tendency to ask questions and seek reasons for the things one is told, the ability to understand what is going on in the world, the ability to pursue one's own interests, and the ability to feel that one could and should make an active contribution to society.

Schools are likely to change in various ways in the future. Information technology is already making changes in the classroom and these are likely to increase as equipment becomes cheaper and more available. The Internet is a huge resource which schools can access. An Ofsted study of homework (Weston 1999) suggests that the time is coming when every child will have access to a computer for homework, either because there is one at home or because the school is able to lend each child a portable computer. The Ofsted study found that just under half of the primary school children and 57 per cent of the secondary school children in the study had a computer at home.

The aspect of ICT which is yet to be developed to any extent is the way in which it might take on the role of the teacher in some areas of children's learning. It has the capacity to assess a child's learning within a discrete area and match the findings with appropriate tasks for new learning. This possibility has enormous implications for the role of the teacher.

Another area in which we are likely to see development is in provision for the exceptionally able. There is a sense in which these children have special needs and we need to consider how best to educate them so that they make the most of their gifts.

We may also see a development in foreign language teaching in the primary schools of the future. Many other countries start foreign languages at an earlier stage than we do and although we are currently short of teachers of foreign languages we are likely to find increasing pressure to be more proficient in at least the European languages. The world is becoming smaller in terms of the connections between different places and children need to see themselves as citizens of the world. They also need to see themselves as guardians of the environment.

The world of work is changing and the children in schools today will need not only the ability to use information technology but also skill in working in a team and the ability to learn and find out new information.

Schools will need to place an increasing emphasis on marketing themselves, especially where they are in competition for pupils. Relationships with parents will continue to be important and there is likely to be a continuing need to cope with rapid change.

Reynolds and Cuttance (1992: 179) list the characteristics of ineffective schools which they suggest have many of the characteristics of an insecure person. These include:

- the projection of teachers' inefficiencies onto children and parents as excuses for ineffectiveness;
- we've always done it this way;
- teachers have built walls against outsiders;
- fear of attempting change in case it fails;
- fantasy that change is someone else's job;
- ring fence mentality.

By contrast they make the following comments about the effective schools:

> Perhaps the most powerful and enduring lesson from all the research on effective schools is that the better schools are more tightly linked, structurally, symbolically and culturally – than less effective ones. They operate more as a whole and less as a loose collection of disparate sub-systems. There is a great deal of consistency within and across the major components of the organisation, especially those of the production function – the teaching-learning process.
>
> (Reynolds and Cuttance 1992: 168)

The National Curriculum does not set out any general aims for education but each school now states its aims in the prospectus it sends to parents. Forward (1988: 61–2) suggests the following aims for primary education:

1 To help pupils become knowledgeable and skilful in relevant and enriching ways.
2 To give pupils information gathering skills, including literacy and numeracy, which will enable them to inform themselves as the need arises.
3 To give pupils the skills needed to order, validate, evaluate and interpret information and also to internalise concepts which are vital to good judgement, particularly those which relate to the kind of adult society they are likely to live in.
4 To give pupils opportunities for using information to make rational choices, decisions and judgements. From these activities to foster the ability to think independently and critically

while deepening self-knowledge and understanding their own emotions and needs.

5　To teach children the importance of encompassing all judgements with consideration for others and to promote actively qualities of tolerance, compassion and kindness.

BIBLIOGRAPHY

Alexander, R. (1984) *Primary Teaching*, London: Holt, Rinehart and Winston.

Alexander, R. (1992) *Policy and Practice in Primary Education*, London: Routledge.

Alexander, R., Rose, J. and Woodhead, C. (1992) *Curriculum Organisation and Classroom Practice in Primary Schools*, London: Department of Education and Science.

Askew, M. and William, D. (1995) *Recent Research in Mathematics Education 5–16*, London: HMSO for Ofsted.

Askew, M., Brown, M., Rhodes, V., Johnson, D. and William, D. (1997) *Effective Teachers of Numeracy*, London: King's College.

Atkin, J., Bastiani, J. and Goode, J. (1988) *Listening to Parents*, London: Croom Helm.

Baird, J. (1992) 'Collaborative reflection, systematic enquiry, better teaching', in Russell, R. and Munby, H. (eds) *Teachers and Teaching: From Classroom to Reflection*, London: Falmer.

Bastiani, J. (1989) *Working with Parents: A Whole School Approach*, Windsor: NFER-Nelson.

Beare, H., Caldwell, B. and Millikan, R.H. (1989) *Creating an Excellent School*, London: Routledge.

Beech, J. (1985) *Learning to Read*, London: Croom Helm.

Bennett, S.N. (1976) *Teaching Styles and Pupil Progress*, London: Open Books.

Bennett, S.N. (1985) 'Interaction and achievement in classroom groups', in Bennett, S.N. and Desforges, C. (eds) *Recent Advances in Classroom Research*, Edinburgh: Scottish Academic Press, for the *British Journal of Educational Psychology*, Monograph series No. 2.

Bennett, S.N. and Blundell, D. (1983) 'Quantity and quality of work in rows and classroom groups', *Educational Psychology* 3(2): 93–105.

Bennett, S.N. and Dunne, E. (undated) *Action and Abstract Talk in Classroom Groups*, Exeter: University of Exeter, mimeographed.

Bennett, S.N. and Dunne, E. (1992) *Managing Classroom Groups*, Hemel Hempstead: Simon and Schuster.

Bennett, S.N., Desforges, C., Cockburn, A. and Wilkinson, B. (1984) *The Quality of Pupils' Learning Experiences*, London: Lawrence Erlbaum Associates.

Bennett, S.N., Wragg, E.C., Carre, C.G. and Carter, D.S.G. (1992) 'A longitudinal study of primary teachers' perceived competence in and concerns about National Curriculum implementation', *Research Papers in Education* 7(1): 53–78.

Berkshire County Council (1993) *The School Compact*, Reading: Berkshire County Council.

Berkshire County Council (1997) *Pathways to Life: Personal and Social Education*, Reading: Berkshire County Council.

Besag, V.E. (1989) *Bullies and Victims in Schools*, Buckingham: Open University Press.

Biott, C. (1987) 'Cooperative group work. pupils' and teachers' membership and participation', *Curriculum* 8(2): 5–14.

Blackburn, M. (1992) 'Choice of initial reading material', in Pinsent, P. (ed.) *Language, Culture and Young Children*, London: David Fulton in association with the Roehampton Institute.

Bourne, J. (ed.) (1994) *Thinking Through Primary Practice*, London: Routledge in association with The Open University.

Boydell, D. (1978) *The Primary Teacher in Action*, London: Open Books.

Braddy, S. (1988) 'Personal, social and moral education in the infants school: a practical approach', in Lang, P. (ed.) *Thinking about Personal and Social Education in the Primary School*, Oxford: Blackwell.

Bradley, H., Eggelston, J., Kerry, T. and Cooper, D. (1985) *Developing Pupils' Thinking Through Topic Work: A Starter Course*, Harlow: Longman for the School Curriculum Development Committee.

Brier, J. (1988) 'Developing a structural social development programme in an inner city school', in Lang, P. (ed.) *Thinking about Personal and Social Education in the Primary School*, Oxford: Blackwell.

Broadfoot, P. (1996) 'Do we really need to write it all down? Managing the challenge of National Curriculum assessment at Key Stage 1 and Key Stage 2', in Croll, P. (ed.) *Teachers, Pupils and Primary Schooling*, London: Cassell.

Broadfoot, P. and Pollard, A. (1996) 'Continuity and change in English primary education', in Croll, P. (ed.) *Teachers, Pupils and Primary Schooling*, London: Cassell.

Brophy, J.E. and Good, T.L. (1970) 'Teachers' communication of differential expectations for children's classroom performance; some behavioural data', *Journal of Educational Psychology*, 61: 365–74.

Brophy, J.E. and Good, L. (1986) 'Teacher behaviour and student achievement', in Wittrock, M.C. (ed.) *Handbook of Research on Teaching*, third edition, New York: Macmillan.

Bryant, P. and Bradley, L. (1985) *Children's Reading Problems*, Oxford: Blackwell.

Bussis, A.M., Chittenden, E.A., Amarel, M. and Klausner, E. (1985) *Inquiry into Meaning: An Investigation of Learning to Read*, Hillsdale, New Jersey: Lawrence Erlbaum Associates.

Campbell, J. (ed.) (1993) *Breadth and Balance in the Primary Curriculum*, London: Falmer.

Campbell, J. and Neill, S.R.St.J. (1992) *Teacher Time and Curriculum Manageability*, London: Assistant Masters' and Mistresses' Association.

Carrick-Smith, L. (1985) 'A research project in paired reading', in Topping, K. and Wolfendale, S. (eds) *Parental Involvement in Children's Reading*, London: Croom Helm.

Central Advisory Council for Education (England) (1967) *Children and Their Primary Schools* (The Plowden Report, Vol. 1), London: HMSO.

Charlton, T. (1988) 'Using counselling skills to enhance children's personal, social and academic functioning', in Lang, P. (ed.) *Thinking about Personal and Social Education in the Primary School*, Oxford: Blackwell.

Chazan, M., Laing, A. and Harper, G. (1987) *Teaching Five to Eight-Year-Olds*, Oxford: Blackwell.

Clay, M. (1972) *The Early Detection of Reading Difficulties: A Diagnostic Survey*, London: Heinemann.

Cleave, S. (1988) 'Continuity from pre-school to infant school', in Cohen A. and Cohen, L. (eds) *Early Education: The School Years: A Source Book for Teacher*, London: Paul Chapman.

176

Cohen, A. and Cohen, L. (eds) (1988) *Early Education: The School Years: A Source Book for Teachers*, London: Paul Chapman.

Cohen, L. and Manion, L. (1983) *A Guide to Teaching Practice*, London: Methuen.

Cooper, P. and McIntyre, D. (1996) *Effective Teaching and Learning: Teachers' and Students' Perspectives*, Buckingham: Open University Press.

Cortazzi, M. (1991) *Primary Teaching: How it is*, London: David Fulton.

Cox, T. and Sanders, S. (1994) *The Impact of the National Curriculum on the Teaching of Five-Year-Olds*, London: Falmer.

Craig, I. (ed.) (1990) *Managing the Primary Classroom*, second edition, Harlow: Longman.

Critchley, M. and Critchley, E.A. (1978) *Dyslexia Defined*, London: Heinemann.

Croll, P. (1986) *Systematic Classroom Observation*, London: Falmer.

Croll, P. (1996) *Teachers, Pupils and Primary Schooling*, London: Cassell.

Cullingford, C. (1995) *The Effective Teacher*, London: Cassell.

Cummins, J. and Swain, M. (1986) *Bilingual Children in Education*, Harlow: Longman.

D'Arcy, P. (1973) *1 Reading for Meaning*, London: Hutchinson for the Schools Council.

Dean, J. (1995) *Managing the Primary School*, second edition, London: Routledge.

Dean, J. (1996) *Managing Special Needs in the Primary School*, London: Routledge.

Delamont, S. (ed.) (1987) *The Primary School Teacher*, London: Falmer.

Department for Education (1994) *Code of Practice on the Identification and Assessment of Special Educational Needs*, London: Central Office of Information.

Department for Education (1995) *The National Curriculum*, London: HMSO.

Department for Education and Employment (1998a) *The National Literacy Strategy: Framework for Teaching*, London: DfEE.

Department for Education and Employment (1998b) *Homework: Guidelines for Primary and Secondary Schools*, London: DfEE.

Department for Education and Employment (1998c) *Home-School Agreements: Guidance for Schools*, London: DfEE.

Department of Education and Science (1975) *A Language for Life* (The Bullock Report), London: HMSO.

Department of Education and Science (1978) *Primary Education in England: A Survey by HM Inspectors of Schools*, London: HMSO.

Department of Education and Science (1981) *Language Performance in Schools: Primary Survey Report No. 1*, APU, London: HMSO.

Department of Education and Science (1982) *Mathematics Counts* (The Cockcroft Report), London: HMSO.

Department of Education and Science (1985a) *The Curriculum from 5 to 16*, Curriculum Matters 2, London: HMSO.

Department of Education and Science (1985b) *Education 8 to 12 in Combined and Middle Schools*, London: HMSO.

Department of Education and Science (1985c) *Committee of Enquiry into the Education of Children from Ethnic Minority Groups (Swann Committee Report) Education for All*, Cmnd No. 9453, London: HMSO.

Department of Education and Science (1985d) *Mathematics from 5 to 16*, Curriculum Matters 3, London: HMSO.

Department of Education and Science (1987) *National Curriculum: Task Group on Assessment and Testing: A Report*, London: Department of Education and Science and Welsh Office.

Department of Education and Science (1988) *The Education Reform Act*, London: HMSO.

Department of Education and Science (1989a) *Discipline in Schools: Report of the Committee of Enquiry Chaired by Lord Elton*, London: HMSO.

Department of Education and Science (1989b) *Mathematics in the National Curriculum*, London: HMSO.

Department of Education and Science (1989c) *Statutory Instrument No. 1261 The Education (School Records) Regulations*, London: HMSO.

Desforges, C. (1985) 'Matching tasks to children's attainment', in Bennett, S.N. and Desforges, C. (eds) *Recent Advances in Classroom Research*, Edinburgh: Scottish Academic Press for the *British Journal of Educational Psychology*.

Desforges, C. and Cockburn, A. (1987) *Understanding the Mathematics Teacher: A Study of Practice in First Schools*, London: Falmer.

Docking, J. (1990a) *Primary Schools and Parents: Rights, Responsibilities and Relationships*, London: Hodder and Stoughton.

Docking, J. (ed.) (1990b) *Education and Alienation in the Junior School*, London: Falmer.

Docking, J. (1992) *Managing Behaviour in the Primary School*, London: David Fulton in association with the Roehampton Institute.

Drummond, M.J. (1993) *Assessing Children's Learning*, London: David Fulton.

Duffin, J. (1987) 'The language of primary mathematics', in Preston, M. (ed.) *Mathematics in Primary Education*, London: Falmer.

Dunne, E. and Bennett, S.N. (1990) *Talking and Learning in Groups: Activity Based In-Service and Pre-Service Materials*, London: Routledge.

Edmonds, R.R. (1979) 'Effective schools for the urban poor', *Educational Leadership* 37(1): 15–27.

Edwards, A. and Knight, P. (1994) *Effective Early Years Education: Teaching Young Children*, Buckingham: Open University Press.

Edwards, D. and Mercer, N. (1987) *Common Knowledge*, London: Methuen.

Eggleston, J. (1992) *The Challenge for Teachers*, London: Cassell.

Elliott, J. (1991) *Action Research for Educational Change*, Buckingham: Open University Press.

Elliott, M. (1988) *Keeping Safe: A Practical Guide to Talking with Children*, London: Hodder and Stoughton.

Evans, M. and Wilson, M. (1980) *Education of Disturbed Pupils*, Schools Council Working Paper 65, London: Methuen.

Farnham-Diggory (1992) *The Learning Disabled Child*, Cambridge, Mass.: Harvard University Press.

Fontana, D. (1988) 'Personality and personal development', in Cohen, A. and Cohen, L. (eds) *Early Education: The School Years: A Source Book for Teachers*, London: Paul Chapman.

Forward, B. (1988) *Teaching in the Smaller School*, Cambridge: Cambridge University Press.

Freeman, J. (1979) *Gifted Children*, Lancaster: MTP Press.

Freeman, J. (1998) *Educating the Very Able: Current International Research*, Office for Standards in Education, London: HMSO.

French, J. (1987) 'Language in the primary classroom', in Delamont, S. (ed.) *The Primary School Teacher*, London: Falmer.

Gaine, C. (1987) *No Problem Here: A Practical Approach to Education and 'Race' in White Schools*, London: Hutchinson.

Gaine, C. (1995) *Still no Problem Here*, Stoke-on-Trent, Trentham Books.

Galloway, D. (1990) 'Interaction with children with special educational needs', in Rogers, C. and Kutnick, P. (eds) *The Social Psychology of the Primary School*, London: Routledge.

Galton, M. (1989) *Teaching in the Primary School*, London: David Fulton.

Galton, M. (1995) *Crisis in the Primary Classroom*, London, David Fulton.

Galton, M. (1998) 'Back to consulting the ORACLE', *Times Educational Supplement*, 3 July, p. 24.

Galton, M. and Patrick, H. (eds) (1990) *Curriculum Provision in the Small Primary School*, London: Routledge.

Galton, M. and Simon, B. (eds) (1980) *Progress and Performance in the Primary Classroom*, London: Routledge and Kegan Paul.

Galton, M. and Williamson, J. (1992) *Group Work in the Primary Classroom*, London: Routledge.

Galton, M., Simon, B. and Croll. P. (1980) *Inside the Primary School*, London: Routledge and Kegan Paul.

Gipps, C. (1992) *What We Know About Effective Primary Teaching*, London: The Tufnell Press, The London file: Papers from the Institute of Education, London.

Gipps, C. (1994) 'What we know about effective primary teaching', in Bourne, J. (ed.) *Thinking Through Primary Practice*, London: Routledge in association with The Open University.

Gipps, C., Brown, M., McCallum, B. and McAllister, S. (1995) *Intuition or Evidence*, Buckingham: Open University Press.

Goodman, K. (1973) 'Psycho-linguistic universals in the reading process', in Smith, F. (ed.) *Psycho-linguistics and Reading*, New York: Holt, Rinehart and Winston.

Gurnah, A. (1987) 'Gatekeepers and caretakers: Swann, Scarman and the social policy of containment', in Troyna, B. (ed.) *Racial Equality in Education*, London: Tavistock Publications.

Gurney, P. (1990) 'The enhancement of self-esteem in junior classrooms', in Docking, J. (ed.) *Education and Alienation in the Junior School*, London: Falmer.

Hammond, J. (ed.) (1998) *Developing Children's Writing*, Leamington Spa: Scholastic.

Hargreaves, L. (1990) 'Teachers and pupils in small schools', in Galton, M. and Patrick, H. (eds) *Curriculum Provision in the Small Primary School*, London: Routledge.

Harwood, D. (1988) 'Personal and social education through cooperative and developmental group work in the primary school: questions for research and development', in Lang, P. (ed.) *Thinking about Personal and Social Education in the Primary School*, Oxford: Blackwell.

Hegarty, S., Pocklington, K. and Lucas, D. (1981) *Educating Pupils with Special Needs in the Ordinary School*, Windsor: NFER-Nelson.

Hewison, J. (1985) 'Parental involvement in reading attainment: implications of research in Dagenham and Haringey', in Topping, K. and Wolfendale, S. (eds) *Parental Involvement in Children's Reading*, London: Croom Helm.

Holt, J. (1984) *How Children Fail*, Harmondsworth: Penguin.

Holt, J. (1994) 'How children learn and fail', in Pollard A. and Bourne, J. (eds) *Teaching and Learning in the Primary School*, London: Routledge.

Hopkins, D. (1993) *A Teacher's Guide to Classroom Research*, second edition, Buckingham: Open University Press.

Houlton, D. (1988) 'Teachers and diversity', in Cohen, A. and Cohen, L. (eds) *Early Education: The School Years: A Source Book for Teachers*, London: Paul Chapman.

Hoyle, E. and Wilks, J. (1974) *Gifted Children and their Education*, London: Department of Education and Science.

Hughes, B. (1987) 'Calculators and computers', in Preston, M. (ed.) *Mathematics in Primary Education*, London: Falmer.

Hughes, M., Wikeley, F. and Nash, T. (1994) *Parents and their Children's Schools*, Oxford: Blackwell.

Johnson, D.W. and Johnson, R.T. (1985) 'The internal dynamics of cooperative learning groups', in Slavin, R. (ed.) *Learning to Cooperate, Cooperating to Learn*, New York: Plenum.

Jones, J. (1993) *School Governors: What Governors need to Know 3*, London, David Fulton.

179

Jungnitz (1985) 'A paired reading project with Asian families', in Topping, K. and Wolfendale, S. (eds) *Parental Involvement in Children's Reading*, London: Croom Helm.

Kelly, A. (1988) 'Gender differences in teacher–pupil interaction: a meta-analytic review', *Research in Education* 39: 1–23.

Kerry, T. (1981) 'Talking: the teacher's role', in Sutton, C. (ed.) *Communicating in the Classroom*, London: Hodder and Stoughton.

Kounin, J. (1970) *Discipline and Group Management in Classrooms*, New York: Holt, Rinehart and Winston.

Kutnick, P. (1990) 'Social development of the child and the promotion of autonomy', in Rogers, C. and Kutnick, P. (eds) *The Social Psychology of the Primary School*, London: Routledge.

Kyriacou, C. (1986) *Effective Teaching in Schools*, Oxford: Blackwell.

Kyriacou, C. (1991) *Essential Teaching Skills*, Oxford: Blackwell.

Lang, P. (ed.) (1988) *Thinking about Personal and Social Education in the Primary School*, Oxford: Blackwell.

Lang, P. (1990) 'Responding to dissaffection: talking about pastoral care in the primary school', in Docking, J. (ed.) *Education and Alienation in the Junior School*, London: Falmer.

Macbeth, A. (1989) *Involving Parents*, London: Heinemann Educational.

Macbeth, A. (1994) 'Involving parents', in Pollard, A. and Bourne, J. (eds) *Teaching and Learning in the Primary School*, London: Routledge.

McConkey, R. (1985) *Working with Parents: A Practical Guide for Teachers and Therapists*, London: Croom Helm.

Maltby, F. (1984) *Gifted Children and Teachers in the Primary School 5–12*, London: Falmer.

Maxwell, W. (1990) 'The nature of friendship in the primary school', in Rogers, C. and Kutnick, P. (eds) *The Social Psychology of the Primary School*, London: Routledge.

Medley D. (1979) 'The effectiveness of teachers', in Peterson, P. and Walberg, H. (eds) *Research on Teaching Concepts, Findings and Implications*, Berkeley, Calif.: McCutchan.

Medwell, J., Wray, D., Poulson, L. and Fox, R. (1998) *Effective Teachers of Literacy: A Report of a Research Project Commissioned by the Teacher Training Agency*, Exeter: University of Exeter.

Millard, E. (1994) *Developing Readers in the Middle Years*, Buckingham: Open University Press.

Miller, L. (1996) *Towards Reading*, Buckingham: Open University Press.

Monk, J. and Karavis, S. (1996) 'Assessment', in Reid, D. and Bentley, D (eds) *Reading on: Developing Reading at Key Stage 2*, Leamington Spa: Scholastic.

Montgomery, D. (1990) *Special Needs in Ordinary Schools: Children with Learning Difficulties*, London: Cassell.

Morgan, N. and Saxton, J. (1991) *Teaching Questioning and Learning*, London: Routledge.

Morgan, R. (1992) 'Distinctive voices – developing oral language in multilingual classrooms', in Pinsent, P. (ed.) *Language, Culture and Young Children*, London: David Fulton in association with the Roehampton Institute.

Mortimore, P., Sammons, P., Stoll, L., Lewis, D. and Ecob, R. (1988) *School Matters*, London: Open Books.

Moyles, J. (1992) *Organising for Learning in the Primary Classroom*, Buckingham, Open University Press.

Muschamp, Y. (1996) 'Pupil self-assessment', in Pollard, A. (ed.) *Readings for Reflective Teaching in the Primary School*, London: Cassell.

Muschamp, Y., Pollard, A. and Sharp, R. (1992) 'Curriculum management in primary schools', *The Curriculum Journal* 3(1): 21–39.

Nash, J. (1973) *Classrooms Observed*, London: Routledge and Kegan Paul.

National Literacy Project (1996) *Framework for Teaching* (Draft), Reading: National Centre for Literacy and Numeracy.

National Literacy Trust (1998) *A Literacy Guide for School Governors*, London: National Literacy Trust.

National Numeracy Project (1997) *Framework for Numeracy Years 1 – 6* (Draft), Reading: National Centre for Literacy and Numeracy.

Needham, J. (1994) 'An approach to social and personal education in the primary school; or how one city schoolteacher tried to make sense of her job', in Pollard, A. and Bourne, J. (eds) *Teaching and Learning in the Primary School*, London: Routledge.

Neill, S. and Caswell, C. (1993) *Body Language for Competent Teachers*, London: Routledge.

Nias, J. (1989) *Primary Teachers Talking: A Study of Teaching as Work*, London: Routledge.

Nuttall, D., Goldstein, H., Prosser, R. and Rasbash, J. (1989) 'Differential school effectiveness', *International Journal of Educational Research*, 13(7): 769–76.

Ofsted (1994a) 'Successful topic work', in Pollard, A. and Bourne, J. (eds) *Teaching and Learning in the Primary School*, London: Routledge.

Ofsted (1994b) *Primary Matters*, London: HMSO.

Ofsted (1996) *Subjects and Standards: Issues for School Development from Ofsted Inspection Findings 1994–5, Key Stages 1 and 2*, London: HMSO.

Olweus, D. (1993) *Bullying at School: What We Know and What We Can Do*, Oxford: Blackwell.

Osborn, M. (1996) 'Teachers mediating change: Key Stage 1 revisited', in Croll, P. (ed.) *Teachers, Pupils and Primary Schooling*, London: Cassell.

Ouston, J. and Maughan, B. (1985) 'Issues in the assessment of school outcomes', in Reynolds, D. (ed.) *Studying School Effectiveness*, London: Falmer.

Perrott, E. (1982) *Effective Teaching: A Practical Guide to Improving your Teaching*, Harlow: Longman.

Perrott, E. (1996) 'Using questions in classroom discussion', in Pollard, A. (ed.) *Readings for Reflective Teaching in the Primary School*, London: Cassell.

Pinsent, P. (ed.) (1992) *Language, Culture and Young Children*, London: David Fulton in association with the Roehampton Institute.

Pollard, A. (1985) *The Social World of the Primary School*, London: Holt, Rinehart and Winston.

Pollard, A. (ed.) (1994) *Look Before You Leap: Research Evidence for the Curriculum at Key Stage 2*, London: The Tufnell Press.

Pollard, A. (ed.) (1996a) *Readings for Reflective Teaching in the Primary School*, London: Cassell.

Pollard, A. (1996b) *An Introduction to Primary Education: for Parents, Governors and Student Teachers*, London: Cassell.

Pollard, A. (1996c) 'Playing the system? Pupil perspectives on curriculum, pedagogy and assessment in primary schools', in Croll, P. (ed.) *Teachers, Pupils and Primary Schooling*, London: Cassell.

Pollard, A. and Bourne, J. (1994) (eds) *Teaching and Learning in the Primary School*, London: Routledge.

Pollard, A. and Tann, S. (1987) *Reflective Teaching in the Primary School*, London: Cassell Education.

Pollard, A., Osborn, M., Abbott, D., Broadfoot, P. and Croll, P. (1993) 'Balancing priorities: children and the curriculum in the nineties', in Campbell, J. (ed.) *Breadth and Balance in the Primary Curriculum*, London: Falmer.

Preston, M. (ed.) (1987) *Mathematics in Primary Education*, London: Falmer.

Pring, R. (1988) 'Personal and social education in the primary school', in Lang, P. (ed.) *Thinking about Personal and Social Education in the Primary School*, Oxford: Blackwell.

Purkey, S.C. and Smith, M.S. (1985) 'The district policy implications of the effective school', *The Elementary School Journal* 85(3): 353–89.

Qualifications and Curriculum Authority (1999) *Assessment and Reporting Arrangements Key Stage 2*, London: Qualifications and Curriculum Authority Publications.

Raven, J., Johnstone, J. and Varley, T. (1985) *Opening the Primary Classroom*, Edinburgh: The Scottish Council for Research in Education.

Reid, D. and Bentley, D. (eds) (1996) *Reading on: Developing Reading at Key Stage 2*, Leamington Spa: Scholastic.

Reid, K., Hopkins, D. and Holly, P. (1987) *Towards the Effective School*, Oxford: Blackwell.

Reynolds, D. (ed.) (1985) *Studying School Effectiveness*, London: Falmer.

Reynolds, D. and Cuttance, P. (eds) (1992) *School Effectiveness Research: Policy and Practice*, London: Cassell.

Reynolds, D. and Reid, K. (1985) 'The second stage: towards a reconceptualisation of theory and methodology in school effectiveness research', in Reynolds, D. (ed.) *Studying School Effectiveness*, London: Falmer.

Reynolds, D., Creemers, B.P.M., Nesselrodt, P.S., Schaffer, E.C., Stringfield, S. and Teddlie, C. (eds) (1994) *Advances in School Effectiveness Research and Practice*, Oxford: Pergamon.

Richards, C. (1987) 'Primary education in England: an analysis of some recent issues and developments', in Delamont, S. (ed.) *The Primary School Teacher*, London: Falmer.

Rogers C. (1990a) 'Motivation in the primary years', in Rogers, C. and Kutnick, P. (eds) *The Social Psychology of the Primary School*, London: Routledge.

Rogers, C. (1990b) 'Disaffection in the junior years: a perspective from theories of motivation', in Docking, J. (ed.) *Education and Alienation in the Junior School*, London: Falmer.

Rogers, C.R. (1961) *On Becoming a Person*, London: Constable.

Rollisson, K. (1990) 'Organising for effective learning', in Craig, I. (ed.) *Managing the Primary Classroom*, second edition, Harlow: Longman.

Romberg, T.A. and Carpenter, T.P. (1986) 'Research on teaching and learning mathematics: two disciplines of scientific enquiry', in Wittrock, M.C. (ed.) *Handbook of Research on Teaching*, third edition, New York: Macmillan.

Rosenshine, B.V. and Stevens, R. (1986) 'Teaching functions', in Wittrock, M.C. (ed.) *Handbook of Research on Teaching*, third edition, New York: Macmillan.

Rosenshine, B.V. and Furst, J. (1971) *Teacher Behaviour and Student Progress*, Slough: National Foundation for Educational Research.

Rosenthal, R. and Jacobson, L. (1968) *Pygmalion in the Classroom*, New York: Holt, Rinehart and Winston.

Rowe, M.B. (1974) 'Wait-time and rewards as instructional variables, their influence on language, logic and fate control: Part 1 Wait-time', *Journal of Research in Science Teaching* 11(2): 81–94.

Rowlands, V. and Birkett, K. (1992) *Personal Effectiveness for Teachers*, Hemel Hempstead: Simon and Schuster.

Russell, R. and Munby, H. (eds) (1992) *Teachers and Teaching: From Classroom to Reflection*, London: Falmer.

Rutter, M., Maughan, B., Mortimore, P. and Ouston, J. (1979) *Fifteen Thousand Hours: Secondary Schools and Their Effects on Children*, London: Open Books.

Sammons, P. and Mortimore, P. (1990) 'Pupil achievement and pupil alienation in the junior school', in Docking, J. (ed.) *Education and Alienation in the Junior School*, London: Falmer.

Sammons, P., Hillman, J. and Mortimore, P. (1995) *Key Characteristics of Effective Schools: A Review of Effectiveness Research*, London: Institute of Education and Ofsted.

Sammons, P., Lewis, A., MacLure, M., Riley, J., Bennett, N.S. and Pollard, A. (1994) 'Teaching and learning processes', in Pollard, A. (ed.) *Look Before You Leap? Research Evidence for the Curriculum at Key Stage 2*, London: The Tufnell Press.

Scheerens, J. (1992) *Effective Schooling: Research, Theory and Practice*, London: Cassell.

Schunk, D.H. (1983) 'Ability versus effort attributional feedback on children's perceived self-efficacy and achievement' *Journal of Educational Psychology* 74.

Schunk, D.H. (1990) 'Self-concept and school achievement', in Rogers, C. and Kutnick, P. (eds) *The Social Psychology of the Primary School*, London: Routledge.

Select Committee on Race Relations and Immigration (1980–81) London: HMSO.

Slavin, R. (1990) 'Cooperative learning', in Rogers, C. and Kutnick, P. (eds) *The Social Psychology of the Primary School*, London: Routledge.

Smith, F. (ed.) (1973) *Psycho-linguistics and Reading*, New York: Holt, Rinehart and Winston.

Smith, F. (1978) *Reading*, London: Cambridge University Press.

Sotto, E. (1994) *When Teaching Becomes Learning: A Theory and Practice of Teaching*, London: Cassell.

Southgate, V., Arnold, H. and Johnson, S. (1981) *Extending Beginning Reading*, London: Heinemann for the Schools Council.

Spear, E. (1990) 'Record keeping', in Craig, I. (ed.) *Managing the Primary Classroom*, second edition, Harlow: Longman.

Stacey, M. (1991) *Parents and Teachers Together*, Buckingham: Open University Press.

Stevenson, C. (1992) 'Language and learning in the multi-cultural nursery', in Pinsent, P. (ed.) *Language, Culture and Young Children*, London: David Fulton in association with the Roehampton Institute.

Stoll, L. and Fink, D. (1996) *Changing our Schools*, Buckingham: Open University Press.

Surrey County Council (1975) *Home and School*, Kingston: Surrey County Council.

Sutton, C. (ed.) (1981) *Communicating in the Classroom*, London: Hodder and Stoughton.

Sylva, K. and Hurry, J. (1995) *Early Intervention in Children with Reading Difficulties: An Evaluation of Reading Recovery and Phonological Training*, London: School Curriculum and Assessment Authority.

Tann, C.S. (1981) 'Grouping and group work', in Simon, B. and Willcocks, J. (eds) *Practice in the Primary Classroom*, London: Routledge and Kegan Paul.

Tansley, P. and Panckhurst, J. (1981) *Children with Specific Learning Difficulties*, Windsor: NFER-Nelson.

Thomas, N. (1993) 'Breadth, balance and the National Curriculum', in Campbell, J. (ed.) *Breadth and Balance in the Primary Curriculum*, London: Falmer.

Tizard, B. (1975) *Early Childhood Education: A Review and Discussion of Research in Britain*, Windsor: NFER Publishing Company for the Social Science Research Council.

Tizard B. and Hughes, M. (1984) *Young Children Learning: Talking and Thinking at Home and at School*, London: Fontana.

Tizard, B., Blatchford, P., Burke, J., Farquhar, C. and Plewis, I. (1988) *Young Children at School in the Inner City*, Hove and London: Lawrence Erlbaum Associates.

Topping, K. (1985) 'An introduction to paired reading', in Topping, K. and Wolfendale, S. (eds) *Parental Involvement in Children's Reading*, London: Croom Helm.

Topping, K. and Wolfendale, S. (eds) (1985) *Parental Involvement in Children's Reading*, London: Croom Helm.

Tough, J. (1973) 'The language of young children', in Chazan, M. (ed.) *Education in the Early Years*, Swansea: University College of Swansea and Aberfan Disaster Fund.

Tough, J. (1976) *Listening to Children Talking: A Guide to the Appraisal of Children's Use of Language*, London: Ward Lock in association with Drake Educational Associates.

Troyna, B. (ed.) (1987) *Racial Equality and Education*, London: Tavistock.

Vygotsky, L.S. (1978) *Mind in Society: The Development of Higher Psychological Processes*, edited by Michael Cole, Vera John-Steiner, Sylvia Scribner and Ellen Souberman, Cambridge, Mass.: Harvard University Press.

Waterhouse, P. (1983) *Managing the Learning Process*, Maidenhead: McGraw-Hill.

Webb, R. and Vulliamy, G. (1996) *Roles and Responsibilities in the Primary School – Changing Demands, Changing Practices*, Buckingham: Open University Press.

Welch, J. (1990) 'Alienation in the junior school: the case for gifted children', in Docking, J. (ed.) *Education and Alienation in the Junior School*, London: Falmer.

Weston, P. (Office for Standards in Education) (1999) *Homework: Learning from Practice*, London: HMSO.

Wheldall, K. and Glynn, T. (1989) *Effective Classroom Learning*, Oxford: Blackwell.

Wheldall, K. and Merrett, F. (1984) *Positive Teaching: The Behavioural Approach*, London: Unwin.

Whitaker, P. (1988) 'The person-centred teacher', in Lang, P. (ed.) *Thinking about Personal and Social Education in the Primary School*, Oxford: Blackwell.

Whyte, J. (1988) 'The "hidden curriculum"', in Cohen, A. and Cohen, L. (eds) *Early Education: The School Years: A Source Book for Teachers*, London: Paul Chapman.

Winkley, D. (1990) 'The management of children's emotional needs in the primary school,' in Docking, J. (ed.) *Education and Alienation in the Junior School*, London: Falmer.

Wittrock, M.C. (ed.) (1986) *Handbook of Research on Teaching*, third edition, New York: Macmillan.

Wolfendale, S. and Bryans, T. (1978) *Identification of Learning Difficulties*, Stafford: National Association for Remedial Education.

Wood, D. (1988) *How Children Learn*, Oxford: Blackwell.

Wood, D., McMahon, L. and Cranston, Y. (1980) *Working with Under Fives*, London: Grant McIntyre.

Woods, P. (1994) 'Chances of a lifetime, exceptional educational events', in Bourne, J. (ed.) *Thinking Through Primary Practice*, London: Routledge in association with The Open University.

Woods, P. (1995) *Creative Teachers in Primary Schools*, Buckingham: Open University Press.

Wooster, A. (1988) 'Social skills training in the primary school', in Lang, P. (ed.) *Thinking about Personal and Social Education in the Primary School*, Oxford: Blackwell.

Wragg, E.C. (1993) *Primary Teaching Skills*, London: Routledge.

Wragg, E.C. and Brown, G. (1993) *Explaining*, London: Routledge.

Wright, D. (1985) 'Towards an adequate conception of early years moral development', in Rogers, C. and Kutnick, P. (eds) *The Social Psychology of the Primary School*, London: Routledge.

Yates, S. (1990) 'Implementing English in the National Curriculum', in Coulby, D. and Ward, S. (eds) *The Primary Core National Curriculum: Policy into Practice*, London: Cassell.

INDEX

ability grouping 42, 72, 77–8, 92, 124
able children 77, 129, 130, 136–8, 172
activities, group 94
advanced reading skills 112–13
affective learning 33, 45
age differences 13–14
aims 31
Alexander, R. 72, 80–1, 85
Alexander, R. *et al.* 42, 75, 79
approaches, teaching 62–3, 75–7, 122–5
Askew, M. and William, D. 66, 67, 77–8
Askew, M. *et al.* 30, 121, 123
assessment 32, 142, 152–65; diagnostic 152; evaluative 152; formative 152; peer 158–9; self- 158–9; summative 152; of teacher performance 155
Assessment of Performance Unit (APU) 115
Atkin, J. *et al.* 139–40
attention seekers 27
attitudes 62–3, 132; to mathematics 126
attribution of success or failure 61
audience, matching language to 104; writing for 115–16
auditory discrimination 133

background, social 14–16
Baird, J. 33
Bastiani, J. 144–5, 148–9
Beare, H. *et al.* 3
Beech, J. 27
behaviour 85–7; assessment 154; children's 85–7; modification 35, 89–90; moral 11; on-task 80, 82–3; problems 90–1, 131, 135–6; social 40; teacher 43, 85–7

Bennett, N.S. 25–6, 94
Bennett, N.S. and Blundell, D. 83
Bennett, N.S. and Dunne, E. 20, 78, 92–3, 94, 95, 96, 97, 98–9
Bennett, N.S. and Kell, J. 64–5
Bennett, N.S. *et al.* 30, 32, 58, 93, 125, 135
Berkshire County Council 11, 44, 149–50
Besag, V.E. 48, 49
Biott, C. 95
Blackburn, M. 108
body language 87–9
Boydell, D. 79
Braddy, S. 11, 46
Bradley, H. *et al.* 70–1, 72
Brier, J. 20
Broadfoot, P. 171
Broadfoot, P. and Pollard, A. 20
Brophy, J.E. and Good, L. 42, 52, 66
Bryant, P. and Bradley, L. 107–8
Bullock Report 54, 101, 109, 112
bullying 47–50
Bussis, A.M. *et al.* 112

calculation 122
calculators 127–8
Campbell, J. and Neill, S.R.St.J. 51–2
Carrick-Smith, L.110
Charlton, T. 47–8
Chazan, M. *et al.* 156
check-lists 162
children 9–23; able 129, 130, 136–8; Carribean 41; exceptional 129–38; left-handed 131; middle-class 41; notes on 161; problem 90–1; with special needs 129–36; thinking 125; working-class 41, 103, 129

circle time 11, 12
citizenship 46
class: inquirers 26, 27; meetings 143;
  newsletters 143; social 14–16, 103
classroom: climate 9, 38–50; control
  85–7; environment 60, 84–5, 113;
  management 75–91; organisation
  79; research 166–170; rules 39–40
Clay, M. 134
Cleave, S. 19
climate: of classroom 9, 38–50;
  management 75–91; moral 39
Cockcroft Report 122
Code of Practice for Special
  Educational Needs 132
Cohen, L. and Manion, L. 88
communication: non-verbal 87–9; with
  parents 143–4; skills 35
competition 10, 29, 60
computers 61, 127–8
concepts 62, 121
conferences, individual 21, 114, 115,
  157
confidence 12
confrontation 91
connectionist teachers 121, 122
continuity 31
control in the classroom 85–7
Cooper, P. and McIntyre, D. 13, 30–1,
  36, 39, 41, 68
cooperative work 3, 29, 60, 70, 82,
  92, 93
Cortazzi, M. 28, 29
Cox, T. and Sanders, S. 73
Critchley, M. and Critchley, E.A. 135
Croll, P. 17
cross-curricular work 125–6
Cullingford, C. 24
culture, of children 9
Cummins, J. and Swain, M. 108
counselling 48
curriculum: children's views of 20–1;
  hidden 8, 43–4, 45; inferred 43;
  National 3, 28, 32–3, 50, 51, 52,
  70, 72–3, 102, 104, 107, 108, 114,
  117, 125–6, 132, 139, 156, 160,
  164, 173

D'Arcy, P. 112
Dean, J. 132, 137
Desforges, C. 57–8
Desforges, C. and Cockburn, A. 30,
  43, 123, 124, 125

Delamont, S. 1, 2, 96
development: child 33; moral 11;
  social 19, 154
diagnosis 36, 125, 134
dialect 103, 105
differentiation 77
direct teaching 63–5, 76
discipline 85–7
discovery 63, 121, 122
discussion 33–4, 68–9, 123–4
display 60, 71, 85
Docking, J. 13, 19, 39–40, 42, 90–1,
  111, 114
dominance 88
drafting 116
drama 105
Drummond, M.J. 125, 152, 165
Duffin, J. 126
Dunne and Bennett, S.N. 94–5
dyslexia 135

Edmonds, R.R. 3
education: health 46; moral 11;
  personal and social 44–8; sex 48
Education Reform Act 171
Edwards, A. and Knight, P. 39
Edwards, D. and Mercer, N. 44, 64–5
effective schools 4, 173; teachers 4
effectiveness, criteria 6
Eggleston, J. 24, 43–4
Elliott, M. 48
Elliott, J. 166
Elton Report 19, 85
emotional problems 135–6
English: as a second language 104;
  Standard 102, 103, 105
enrichment of the curriculum 137
environment: classroom 60, 84–5;
  learning 34; organisation of 32, 34;
  study 71
errors, analysing 158
ethnic differences 18–19
evaluation: of classroom research
  169–70; effects of 165; forms of
  156–64; of group work 98–9;
  planning 164; of projects 72; of
  reading 114–15; and record keeping
  152–165
Evans, M. and Wilson, M. 136
exceptional children 129–38
expectation, teacher 40–4
experience: children's 34; first-hand
  23, 53–5, 126

exposition 24, 63, 124
extra-curricular activity 13
eye contact 88, 105

Farnham-Diggory, S. 135
feedback 61–2, 66, 166
fieldwork 71
first-hand experience 23, 53–5, 126
Fontana, D. 10
foreign language teaching 172
Forward, B. 70, 71, 75, 173
Freeman, J. 129–30, 133, 137–8
French, J. 68, 105–6
friendship 19, 20, 46

Gaine, C. 21, 22
Galloway, D. 38–9, 43
Galton, M. 4, 52, 62, 65, 73, 76, 80,
  167–8
Galton, M. and Patrick, H. 76, 95
Galton, M. and Simon, B. 17, 26
Galton, M. and Williamson, J. 95, 96,
  97–8, 99
Galton, M. et al. 26, 82, 93
gender differences 16–18
gifted children 77, 129, 130, 136–8
Gipps, C. 55, 76
Gipps, C. et al. 32, 152–3
goal setting 21
Goodman, K. 108
grammar 118–19
group, activities 94; composition
  94–5; cooperative 3, 29, 60, 70, 82,
  92, 93; coordinator 96; instructors
  26, 27, 29; leadership 96; reading
  112; tasks 97; work 20, 92–100,
  104
grouping 34; by ability 42, 72, 77–8,
  92, 124; friendship 78; for learning
  77–8; mixed ability 78; mixed
  gender 78; types of 93–4
Gurnah, A. 22
Gurney, P. 12, 13, 20

Hammond, J. 115
handwriting 116–17; policy 117
Hargeaves, L. 80
Harwood, D. 93
hearing problems 133
Hegarty, S. et al. 132–3
Hewison, J. 110
hidden 8, 43–4, 45
HMI 124–5

Holt, J. 22, 167
home learning 140
home/school agreements 149–50
home visits 148
homework 73–4, 142–3, 172
Hopkins, D. 166–7, 169–70
Houlton, D. 18
Hoyle, E. and Wilks, J. 137
Hughes, B. 127
Hughes, M. et al. 142, 143, 144

identifying exceptional children
  129–32
individual: interviews 21, 114, 115,
  157; monitors 26, 27; work 2, 76,
  79, 81, 123
ineffective schools 173
Information and Communication
  Technology (ICT) 102, 172
interaction 66; pupil/pupil 19, 40;
  pupil/teacher 17, 79
interactive teaching 63, 69, 123
intermittent workers 27, 28
Internet 23, 70, 138, 172
interviews 21, 114, 115, 168

Johnson, D.W. and Johnson, R.T. 96
Jones, J. 139, 151
Jungnitz, G. 112

Kelly, A. 17
Kerry, T. 69
knowledge: of children 33; children's
  62; of number 122; self- 32; subject
  32; teacher's 32
Kounin, J. 87
Kutnick, P. 22–3
Kyriacou, C. 37, 38, 55–6, 62, 63,
  66, 86, 87–8, 155

Lang, P. 44–5, 46, 50, 131
language 55, 71, 103–4; body 87–9;
  children's 102–6; in the
  environment 107; teacher's 87–8; in
  mathematics 126–7
learning, affective 33, 45; discovery
  63, 64; effective 51–74;
  environment 34; experiential 55–6;
  grouping for 77–8; home 140;
  independent 154; of instruction
  109; motivation for 59–62; oral
  102–6; social 46, 154; structuring
  34, 56–7; styles 26–8

level descriptions 159–60
listening 102–6
literacy: hour 102, 113; policy 102;
    skills 101–2; teaching of 101–19
literature 112

Macbeth, A. 140, 144
McConkey, R. 150–1
Maltby, F.138
management, classroom 75–91
marking 162–3
matching work to children 57–9
mathematics 30, 43, 120–8; practical
    124
Maxwell, W. 19, 20, 46
Medley, D. 52
Medwell, J. et al. 102, 106, 108, 114,
    118
methods, teaching 62–3; 75–7, 122–5
Millard, E. 94, 114, 118
Miller, L. 107
mixed gender groups 20
monitoring 157; performance of
    different groups 154
Monk, J. and Karavis, S. 115
Montgomery, D. 135, 136
moral: behaviour 11; development 11;
    education 11
morality 12
Morgan, R. 104
Morgan, N. and Saxton, J. 67, 69
Mortimore, P. et al. 6, 7, 13–14,
    15–16, 17, 18, 28, 29, 33, 41, 42,
    68, 72, 77, 81, 148
motivation 21, 59–62; intrinsic and
    extrinsic 59
Moyles, J. 41, 53, 83
multicultural education 22
Muschamp, Y. 158–9
Muschamp, Y. et al. 72

narrative 119
Nash, J. 41
National Assessment 159–60
National Curriculum 3, 28, 32–3, 50,
    51, 52, 70, 72–3, 102, 104, 107,
    108, 114, 117, 125–6, 132, 139,
    156, 160, 164, 171, 173
National Literacy Strategy 30, 101–2,
    105
National Literacy Trust 102, 114
National Numeracy Project 120,
    122–3

Needham, J. 19–29, 159
Neill, S. and Caswell, C. 87, 88, 89
Nias, J. 25, 76
non-fiction 113
non-verbal communication 87–9
note-making 113
Numeracy Project 77
Nuttall, D. et al. 8

objectives 31, 34, 64
observation 39–40, 32, 156–7, 166
Ofsted 2, 64, 71, 121, 154, 157, 172
Olweus, D. 48, 49, 50
Oracle study 26, 27, 28, 29, 80, 93
Osborn, M. 73
Ouston, J. and Maughan, B. 8

PACE (Primary Assessment,
    Curriculum and Experience) project
    20, 171
parents: activities involving 144–5;
    communication with 143–4; ethnic
    minority 149; helping in the
    classroom 83–4, 148–9; helping
    with mathematics 128; listening to
    children reading 109–12; as
    partners 141; surveys of 148; views
    of schools and teachers 143;
    working with 139–51
parent/teacher meetings 145–8
pastoral care 45–6
Pathways to Life 11, 44–5
Pause, prompt and praise 110
peer assessment 158–9; tutoring 60–1,
    111
Perrott, E. 51, 65, 66, 67
personal: style 28–9, 52; and social
    education 44–8; and social skills 40,
    45–6, 131, 132, 136
personality 52
personhood 9, 10
phonics 107–8
physical disabilities 132
planning 30–1; long-term 30–1;
    medium-term 30–1; short-term
    30–1
Plowden Report 1, 39, 76
poetry 119
Pollard, A. 3, 21, 38, 39, 52, 59,
    62–3, 64, 77, 159–60
Pollard, A. and Bourne, J. 143, 153
Pollard, A. and Tann, S. 35–6, 38, 62
practical mathematics 124

praise, use of 33, 40, 59, 60, 62, 90
Primary Survey 29, 57, 126
Pring, R. 9
problem-solving 34–5, 60, 122–3
progression 72
projects 69–72
punctuation 118–19
pupil autonomy 22–3
pupil/pupil interaction 19, 40
pupil/teacher interaction 17
Purkey, S.C. and Smith, M.S. 3

Qualifications and Curriculum
    Authority 163, 164
questions: answering 67; distribution
    of 67; higher-order 65; lower-order
    65; open-ended 65; recall 65;
questionnaire surveys 148, 169
questioning 65–7, 103; research into
    167–8; use of pause in 66
quiet collaborators 27

racism 21–2, 49
Raven, J. et al. 3, 171–2
reading 106–15; advanced skills
    112–13; beginning 106–9;
    conferences 114–15; environment
    113–14; group 112; hearing
    109–12, 114; levels 109; paired
    110
Reading Recovery 134
real books approach 108
records 132, 152–165; of achievement
    132, 160–1; children's own 162;
    recording 32, 160
reflection 11, 19, 35–7, 155, 166–70
Reid, D. and Bentley, D. 113
Reid, K. et al. 92, 98
reinforcement 40–4
relationships, social 19–20; pupil/pupil
    19, 45, 46; teacher/pupil 47
reliability of measures 7
reports: to parents 144, 160, 163–4;
    transfer 164
research, assessing 6–8
responsibility 46
reward 35
Reynolds, D. and Cuttance, P. 173
Reynolds, D. and Reid, K. 7
Reynolds, D. et al. 64, 78
rhyming 107
Richards, C. 68–9
Rogers, C. R. 38

Rollisson, K. 84
Romberg, T.A. and Carpenter, T.P. 6,
    54, 56
Rosenshine, B.V. and Furst, J. 64
Rosenshine, B.V. and Stevens, R. 123
Rosenthal, R. and Jacobson, L. 40
Rowe, M.B. 66
Rowlands, V. and Birkett, K. 146
rules: about bullying 49; classroom
    39–40, 50, 87; for discussion 69;
    social 39, 46
Rutter, M. et al. 6

Sammons, P. and Mortimore, P.
    16–17, 18
Sammons, P. et al. 3, 42, 55, 70, 72
Scheerens, J. 3, 56, 78
Schunk, D.H. 12–13, 21
seating 82–3; in groups 82–3; mixed
    sex 83; in rows 82–3
security 10
Select Committee on Race Relations
    and Immigration 22
self-assessment 158–9; concept 12–13,
    17, 47, 133; confidence 45, 131,
    132; esteem 10, 45, 60, 78, 131,
    132, 166; image 47; knowledge 32
    setting 77–8
sex education 48
slow learners, provision for 133–5
skills 62; accessing 71; advanced
    reading 112–13; communication 35;
    comprehension 71; group work 98;
    literacy 101–2; observation 71;
    recording 71; research 71; social 40,
    131, 132, 136; for working with
    parents 150–1
Slavin, R. 94
Smith, F. 108–9
social: background 14–16; behaviour
    40; class 14–16, 103; development
    19, 154; education 44–8; learning
    46, 154, relationships 19–20; skills
    40, 131, 132, 136
solitary workers 2
Sotto, E. 56, 59–60, 64, 65
Southgate, V. et al. 109, 111, 113–14
space, use of 84–5
speaking 102–6
Spear, E. 160
special educational needs 129–38
spelling 117–18, 135
Stacey, M. 146, 149

Standard Assessment Tasks (SATs) 157
standardised tests 157
stereotyping 41
Stevenson, C. 104
Stoll, L. and Fink, D. 3, 4, 35
stress 37
style, changers 26; learning 26–8;
  teaching 25–9
success 13
Survey of Combined and Middle
  Schools 78
Sutton, C. 57, 104–5
Swann Report 21–2
Sylva, K. and Hurry, J. 133

Tann, C.S. 93
Tansley, P. and Panckhurst, J. 134, 135
tape-recordings: of children's work
  162; of lessons 167
target-setting 160
Task Group on Assessment and
  Testing 152
teacher 24–37; creative 4–5, 50;
  connectionist 121–2; the effective 4,
  121–2; expectation 40–4;
  knowledge 32–5; as researcher
  166–70; skills 32–5; tasks 29–32;
  transmissionist 121–2
teaching: approaches 75–7, 122–5;
  assistants 83–4; direct 63–5;
  effective 51–74, 121–2; of foreign
  languages 172; individual 76;
  interactive 63; of literacy 101–19;
  of mathematics 120–8; methods
  62–3; reflective 35–7; style 25–6;
  team 85; whole-class 2, 3, 29, 75,
  81, 123
testing 157–8
Thomas, N. 69–70
time: use of 80–2; children's use of
  81–2; planning 82; teacher's use of
  81–2
Tizard, B. 14–15
Tizard, B. and Hughes, M. 15, 68, 103

Tizard B. et al. 17, 41, 80, 141, 142
tone of voice 88
topic work 69–72
Topping, K. 110, 111
Topping, K. and Wolfendale, S.
  109–10
Tough, J. 14–15, 103–4, 105
transmissionist teachers

validity of measures 7
values 11
voice, tone of 88
Vygotsky, L.S. 58–9, 103, 156

Waterhouse, P. 65
Webb, R. and Vulliamy, G. 23, 31,
  32, 52, 70, 77, 92, 99–100
Welch, J. 131
Weston, P. 172
Wheldall, K. and Glynn, T. 20, 81,
  82, 83, 89, 111
Wheldall, K. and Merritt, F. 35
Whitaker, P. 47, 52
whole-class work 2, 3, 29, 75, 81,
  123; interactive 29
Whyte, J. 16
Winkley, D. 90, 131, 136
Wolfendale and Bryans, T. 133
Wood, D. 56
Wood, D. et al. 103
Woods, P. 3, 4, 50, 54, 69, 72
Wooster, A. 12, 40
word-processing 116
working-class children 41, 103, 129
working in groups 92–100
Wragg, E.C. 36–7, 40
Wragg, E.C. and Brown, G. 63–4
writing 115–19; for audience 115–16;
  stories 116, 119; style 116
Wright, D. 12

Yates, S. 105

zone of proximal development 156